# THE RIPPLE EFFECT OF CHILD SEX ABUSE LAWS

## CAN AND SHOULD CHANGE OCCUR?

DEBRA SUSAN PENROD, PH.D.

ISBN: 979-8-89079-417-8 (paperback)

Jetlaunch Publishing

# ACKNOWLEDGMENTS

I would especially like to thank my immediate family for their continued support and understanding. My office staff has also been a tremendous help to me. Others to thank include Dr. Floyd Robison, my personal mentor and friend. Thank you for keeping me on track and helping me to write what I really wanted to say, only in fewer words. Dr. Gale Vrtiak, who has been extremely patient in helping me to articulate my thoughts on paper. Dr. Steven Daniels and Dr. Norma Ross have been there to answer many questions along the way. My research assistant Jesse Ballinger has also been a great help with the legwork in the library. In addition, I would especially like to thank my editors at Edit 911.

I would like to give a very special thanks to contributors in the legal profession. Your knowledge and opinions were extremely insightful.

I would especially like to thank the survivors of childhood sexual abuse who contributed to this project. I applaud your courage. You are the real heroes. If you are still a victim, work toward becoming a survivor. The work is definitely worth it! Survival is life.

# TABLE OF CONTENTS

Introduction . . . . . . . . . . . . . . . . . . . . . . . . . . . . . . .vii

Chapter 1: Statement of Problem and Position . . . . . . . .1

Chapter 2: Illustrative Case Study: Eve . . . . . . . . . . . . . .6

Chapter 3: Definitions and Characteristics of
            Childhood Sexual Abuse . . . . . . . . . . . . . .27

Chapter 4: The Perpetrator . . . . . . . . . . . . . . . . . . . . . .36

Chapter 5: Impacts of Childhood Sexual Abuse . . . . . . .43

Chapter 6: History of Child Sex Abuse Laws, the
            Legal Process, and Sentencing Procedures. . .85

Chapter 7: Summary and Recommendations . . . . . . . .101

Epilogue: Other Voices Cry Out . . . . . . . . . . . . . . . .109

Bibliography . . . . . . . . . . . . . . . . . . . . . . . . . . . . . . .119

Appendix I: Interview Questions for Criminal
            Justice Personnel . . . . . . . . . . . . . . . . . . . .129

# INTRODUCTION

Through the writing and rewriting of this project, my personal mentor and I decided that the traditional thesis or research paper was not the best way to describe this piece of work. The guidelines and procedures section of the directions say, "a Capstone represents the crowning of a candidate's professional, clinical, academic and other related experience and knowledge." Since I began my career as a therapist, the bulk of my caseload has been related to the problems of adult survivors of childhood sexual abuse. This has not been by design. I am Adlerian in my thought process as a therapist, so I have searched beyond the surface issues with my patients. This has opened up unhealed wounds that relate to everyday life. As we process these unhealed wounds, many patients reveal past sexual abuse, some for the first time in their lives. Most have found relief from disclosure, some have needed to disconnect from their families of origin, and a few have confronted their abusers and found guilt-ridden offenders or mothers wanting forgiveness.

It is due to this bulk of work that I have developed a passion for helping those with this problem. I have also developed strong opinions, hence the need to define this project as a position paper.

When stories of sexual abuse appear in the newspaper or on television news shows, most people, at least in public, seem appalled. But do our laws reflect that emotion? Currently, our laws punish offenders less for molestation than for armed robbery. Recently, someone made headlines for advertising illegally on the internet (SPAM). His sentence was nine years in prison. Sentencing for child molesters ranges from probation or work release to life in prison, depending upon the extent of the abuse. For example, in most states, fondling of a child by an adult for sexual pleasure carries a sentence of about one year in jail or work release and one to three years probation (Legal Information Institute, 2004). What does this mean? Are possessions or money or even screen time more important than the innocence of a child? In a free society, our laws should represent our cultures' social mores. It is my opinion that the general public is not aware of the immediate or long-term effects to victims. This is a subject that has long been ignored, or just swept under the rug by the supposed protectors of the victims and their families. Are child molesters treatable? Does sexual abuse of children tend to continue in families over time? Is there a "ripple effect" through the families of victims? Is there a "ripple effect" for society? These questions will be addressed through the research in this paper.

The avenues through which my position will be supported include: one family's in-depth case study, the opinions of professionals in the legal system, the writings of those specializing in this field and the voices of victims and survivors. A traditional literature review separate from the body of the work will not be needed. Research from published literature will be used throughout the paper. Since most of the current literature concerns the sexual abuse of females, this project will deal primarily with the childhood sexual abuse of females.

# CHAPTER 1

## STATEMENT OF
## PROBLEM AND POSITION

**D**irectional Hypothesis: Child sexual abuse penalties should be significantly more rigorous in order to prevent an individual who is not likely to be rehabilitated from offending again. Furthermore, our current legal system does not punish offenders relative to the serious impact perpetrated upon the victims.

The background information to follow will show that re-offending is the norm not an exception. The forthcoming research will also show the significant and lifelong problems suffered by the victims. The "ripple effects", or continued consequences for the families of the victims and society as a whole will be evident.

Current literature indicates that there is much discrepancy between reported vs. non-reported cases and substantiated vs. non-substantiated cases. One very significant statistic is the percentage increase of reported cases of childhood sexual abuse from 1980 to 1990 -- a staggering 322 percent. It is also estimated that there are sixty million survivors of childhood sexual abuse in America today, 27 percent women and 16 percent men. It is also reported that the average child sex offender has molested 115 victims before they are subject to any legal consequences (APRI, 2004).

If the public were made aware of the prevalence and the consequences of childhood sexual abuse, would the laws change?

After much study, the most common averages suggested are that one out of every three girls and one out of every six boys are molested before they reach the age of 18. Even if these statistics are off a bit, they are still staggering. Finding statistics of how many homes contain a molester proved to be impossible. Perhaps, this is a statistic that the general public would not like to hear. Reports indicate that most children who are victimized are abused by someone in their own household. Let us just suppose, based on the above statistics, that an average of one out of every 5-7 households contains a molester. While this statistic brings the problem home just a bit more and possibly makes the situation more realistic to the general public, no one wants to think that a molester may be among their midst. Even so, child molesters are everywhere. We work with them, play ball with them, play cards with them, go to PTA with them, drink with them and go to church with them. In addition, we let our children stay the night at their homes. As long as we meet the parents and they seem nice, we assume, it must be OK to leave our children in their midst. This seems logical, right? Think again and think hard. There is no real profile for a molester, they cross all racial, religion and financial lines. Extensive research shows that sexual abuse has always been prevalent in society, but it has been swept under the rug, ignored, or maybe some men believe they have the right to please themselves sexually with any female in their household. Perhaps, this is a way for men to show their power and dominance because they feel inadequate and small around their own peers. Perhaps, they are just "small, little, men," who are afraid of real adults, and they need to prey upon children to maintain a feeling of adequacy. Alternatively, they may have become desensitized to the negative effects caused by adult to child sexual perpetration; perhaps their own molestation, now, seems normal to them. In our case study with Eve, she heard her father say, in open court, that he did not know he was doing anything wrong.

The regularity of incest and other forms of molestation is frightening. Statistics involving individuals who were molested as children show that they are more likely to become perpetrators of that same abuse. When their own abuse has become their norm, they are socialized into that adult role of abuser. If they believe what happened to them was normal they are less likely to believe that they suffer from some sort of pathology. They feel as though repeating their own traumatic experience is a way to overcome their past (Abramson, Pinkerton, 2001).

Much of the material studied reports that society is trying to take a stand against sexual abuse and it are now intervening. On the other hand, is it only token intervention -- an action meant to calm those who cry for justice? Perhaps, this study will shed light on this issue as well.

If these families are not recognized and help is not provided, will this problem impact society as a whole? If families make up society and the statistics above are true and the ramifications to victims and families are real, what kind of society, other than a decadent one, can be expected? Just imagine if this one issue was eradicated, or at least deterred. In what kind of world would we live?

What responsibility does society have in recognizing these families, or what responsibility does society have in helping these families? If not helped, what does this mean for our society? Does our government not have a responsibility to protect our children? If the previously discussed statistics are correct, our government is failing miserably. Could it be that this failure is due to the public's failure to break the silence concerning sexual abuse? Survivors need to talk loud enough for people to know about the consequences suffered. Mother's Against Drunk Driving (MADD) originated out of someone's pain and suffering. As others began to join in and talk about their own agony, a wave of concern and interest began. Laws changed because of public outcry. The outcry of survivors of sexual abuse could have that same impact, but the silence must be broken. Others who suspect sexual abuse also need to break their silence. Eyes must be opened.

> Incest is there. It has always been. You could not see it because the light was not shining in the right direction, someone was blocking it, or you avoided looking. It is time to shine the light so we transform the lives of children and adult survivors of childhood sexual abuse and incest (Lev, 2003).

When the effects of a particular event are brought into the daylight and examined, the truth must be faced, unless one chooses to continue to live in denial. Incest is among the worst forms of sexual abuse because it destroys the family's trust in one another. The victims are not only angry with their abusers, but with other members of the family, as well, for failing to protect them (Stark, Holly, 1988).

As described by Eby (2004), the trauma of sexual abuse may delimit or interfere with ongoing cognitive development needed for regular childhood tasks. Physical reality is clearly tied to problem solving and this skill can become extremely challenging, especially for a child who is at the mercy of an authority figure, whose only goal is to satisfy his or her own sexual needs. A rule system of understanding must be developed as the process of operational thought is developed. The secrecy, suppression, and denial demanded interferes with this understanding. The development of social cognition involves the child's own needs and perceptions being differentiated from others. Again, this is not possible when the needs of the abusers are paramount. "Abuse is a blatant distortion in the child's sense of power" (Eby, 2004).

Bass and Davis (1988) also described the effects of childhood sexual abuse. The behaviors that parents and professionals should watch for are depression, panic/anxiety attacks, anger, inability to trust, low self-esteem, crying frequently, nightmares, mood swings, intimacy problems, flashbacks, fears, confusion, feeling crazy, guilt, grief, isolation, shame, and despair.

These symptoms may appear without apparent reason, but should be treated as real. They are very real to the child.

**Sub-Positions:**

1) Child sexual abuse permanently, dramatically and adversely impacts victims' lifelong functioning.

2) Most adult child sexual abusers are untreatable.

3) Child sex offenders are likely to re-offend despite the implementation of our current legal sentencing guidelines.

4) Child sex offenders are likely to re-offend under our current legal procedures for sentence modification.

# CHAPTER 2

## ILLUSTRATIVE CASE STUDY: EVE

The following is the case study of one specific survivor, a survivor who is willing to defy societal norms and tell "the family secrets." We will call her Eve. Eve will not only reveal the incest and other sexual deviance in her family, but also her dealings with the legal system. The goal is to determine the "ripple effect," if any, throughout this family and of those around them and if this "ripple effect" is consequential for society. The real names and real places will remain anonymous in this illustration. You may think you know Eve, and maybe you do. There are many Eve's all around us; some crying for help, some crying in silence. How will you respond?

Basic Information & Clinical Diagnosis:

Eve    Age 48    Profession: Health Field
Income Level: $150,000    Married 27 years with two adult sons
Education Level: Master's Degree
Axis I    309.81 Post Traumatic Stress Disorder,
          300.02 Generalized Anxiety,
          296.3 Chronic Depression,
          314.01 Adult Attention Deficit Hyperactivity Disorder,

300.6 Depersonalization Disorder (stabilized).
Axis II  V71.09 No Diagnosis
Axis III  Fibromyalgia, Asthma, Arthritis, Reflux Esphogitis,
Degenerative Disease, Complicated Migraines,
Irritable Bowel Syndrome, Kidney Stones, as per
MD reports
Axis IV  Stress and Anxiety due to PTSD and Chronic Pain
Axis V  GAF = 59
Medical Prognosis -- Poor
Mental Prognosis -- Good

Eve's Story, in her own words:

"What is normal? This question has plagued most
of my life, especially my childhood. I would watch
other families at church, at softball games, and other
social events wondering what family secrets they had
to carry. At some point, I must have decided that little
girls were the ones who had to keep the secrets because
I prayed to God that I would never give birth to a
daughter. I, now, have two sons. God answered that
prayer. Why did I not pray for the abuse to stop? I
guess that I thought that **it** was normal. **He** told me
that **it** was normal. I trusted **him**, believed **him** and at
one time loved **him**. Why not; **he** was my father.

Most of my extended family will not understand
nor approve of my revelations, but "handling it"
within the family did not work twenty three years ago
and it is not going to work now. Besides, it should
not be my "dirty" secret to carry. Molestation continues in many families and will continue without check
until we (the survivors) get the courage to speak up.
Very few people have any idea of the pain, shame and
extreme low self-esteem that we carry for the rest of

7

our lives, therefore, I have decided not to remain silent any longer. The following is a condensed version of my life to the best of my recollection. By the age of five I knew that I was afraid of my father. I was not sure why. I only knew that I did not want to be left alone with him. My earliest memory of shame was on a warm autumn afternoon. My parents had just bought a new electric blanket. For some reason, my mother had left for a short time and (I am not sure where my younger brother was) I was alone with my father. I remember being in my parent's bed with him when my mother came home unexpectedly. Why I felt ashamed, I'm not sure. But when mom asked what we were doing in bed in the middle of the afternoon, I was. I do know now (as an adult) that I am afraid of electric blankets.

My family lived in a small house out by the high-way. My brother and I shared a room. I slept on the top bunk and prayed each night that the "big hand" would not come. When it did come, I would awaken feeling as though I would suffocate with the "big hand" over my face. I am not sure what was happening during these episodes. I learned at a young age to dissociate my mind from my body. Life was easier that way. Our house was always busy. Because my mother was a child-care provider, I was afraid for those children, but I had no power to change anything. I returned to the house a few years ago, even then, it made me shiver. It was suffocating!

When I was in the fourth grade, we moved to a larger house, not far away. I got my own room, but I missed my brother. If you looked at our family from the outside, it looked perfectly normal. Mom was still babysitting and was at home, Dad worked, providing financially for the family. We were always in church, Sunday morning and night. My father was a song leader. In fact, when other churches had revivals, he led songs for them. My brother and I were trained singers and were "paraded" from church to church as a family quartet. My father was so proud. I liked singing, but I was very confused about religion. My father seemed to be admired in the church. When he read the Bible aloud on Sundays, I wondered why he had me read him stories from the Porno magazines. I did not understand most of what I read, but Dad seemed to like it. Even today, as I write this, I can still see his erection and hear him tell me it was his duty as my father to teach me these things. He "didn't want me to learn them from strangers." I felt less than human. Maybe, I was his property like one of the farm animals. I guess Mom must have approved, or at least was in denial. She encouraged me to go upstairs to "rub your dad's head, he has a headache and you know what to do." While rubbing his head, he would rub my chest and if I tried to leave or say that I didn't like it, he would tell me how good it felt and how these acts were what I was supposed to be doing. Mom would be downstairs watching old movies. I still hate old movies!

When I started to develop breasts, I tried to hide them. In fact, I tried to hide completely, and I was successful. However, in striving to hide from my father, I also hid from myself. Between the ages twelve to fourteen, they are a blur. I pray they remain a blur, for because at this point in my life, I do not want to remember! When I was fourteen, my mother gave birth to my youngest brother. She was sick right after his birth. I took care of the baby at night. It was easier to take care of him, if he just slept with me; *he saved me.*

From that point on, my negative past was blocked from my mental consciousness. I still knew that I was afraid of my dad, but I did not remember why for another ten years.

When I was twenty-five years old, by then married and living with my husband and our oldest son, I was told rumors were going around that my father had "touched" one of the little girls under the care of my mother. This news hit me so hard that I was sick for days. The next few months as my memories started to flow were some of the most painful of my life. I tried seeking counseling, but never found anyone with whom I could really talk. I could not find anyone who really understood what or how I felt. My husband and friends from church were my sounding boards.

At first, I thought I needed to remain silent, but after much agonizing, I knew I needed to tell other members of my family, but I was afraid of what their reactions would be. Finally, my need to disclose over-powered my fear. I carefully picked out family members who I thought would try to look past the stigma and truly want to help. After all, I was not the first one to suggest this about my father, and I had hoped their love for me would give them the courage to stand up and do what was right (whatever that might be) in order that no one else be hurt. I could not have been more wrong! The one relative that I thought believed me and had promised that the family would take care of things; disappointed me the most. I found out later she thought I was crazy, as did everyone else in whom I had confided. When my mother called me a liar, accusing me of trying to rip the family apart, I stopped talking while crawling back into my shell. I spent the next twenty years as the family outcast. I attended family functions playing the dutiful daughter, but I knew that I was still on the outside looking in. During this time, I experienced numerous health and emotional problems.

I got a call on January 1, 2000 telling me another member of the family had told someone my father had molested her. I again took on the guilt myself. "If only I had told more people," if only "I had yelled louder, if only I had kept screaming until someone would listen." My brothers and I spent most of the night of 1/1/00 talking, crying and comparing memories.

It seemed as though we each had a different set of parents. My youngest brother (fourteen years younger) had felt loved and cared for while having no idea that our family was dysfunctional. His greatest emotion seemed to be deep sadness and anger. He and I were practically inseparable until he was about six years old, when I went off to college. I had tried to stay close to him, but coming to see him meant I had to see my parents, and while not yet experiencing my memories, I still did not visit often. When my brother was about ten years old, he thought I had done something to hurt our parents, so we were not close for the next twenty years, which coincided with the time of my short period of disclosure and confrontation. When my "baby" brother found out he had lost twenty years of being close to his sister, the one he had adored when he was young, because of lies, secrets and sexual abuse, he sat at my feet and cried. "They took you away from me!" I will never forget the look on his face as he wept. At this time, he was expecting his first child; a daughter. The following week he called me, franticly asking, if he would or could become a molester like our father. I HATE that he had to experience that thought and that kind of pain. I assured him this was not a genetic problem. When I see him now with his beautiful 3-year-old little girl, I am in awe of the love he showers over her, and her love for him is exuberant. I do not understand this kind of father/daughter relationship, but I thank God that it (really) does exist. We are so much closer now, I cry every time my beautiful, bright, loving niece leaves from a visit with us and when I think about her. It makes me ill that she lives minutes from my father's house.

My other brother, three years younger than me had (yet) a different set of parents. As a child, he was adored by his mother, loved by his father, but treated very harshly by him. He worked very hard to please our father; especially in sports. I used to dread coming home from basketball games. Dad would yell and demean him over every mistake that Dad thought my brother had made during the game.

My brother was a great athlete, but the mental abuse he endured to become one could not have been worth it. There were those times when discipline crossed the line. I do not think being pelted with ears of corn from close range would be considered appropriate, then or now. While my youngest brother and I were crying and finding each other again, my other brother was trying to be rational while coming up with a logical plan. I had told him about our father twenty years earlier, but his memory of this conversation was a bit fuzzy considering it was an extremely difficult period of his life. He had been going through a divorce with child custody issues. I am sure that my "crazy" accusations were the least of his worries. Although, I need him to remember, for my validation, he needs to forget, in order not to feel the guilt. I hold no ill-will towards him; I love both of my brothers and now understand how, while living in the same household, we each had different parents in their treatment of us. The set of parents I had were emotionally, physically and sexually abusive. It took me years of study to learn that my mother's abusive behaviors, mostly emotional, though not all, were because she also grew up in a dysfunctional family, and then married a man who preferred young girls sexually, so, why would she want me around? The disturbing question is, if she knew what he was, or even suspected what or who he was, then "why" was she a caretaker to the children of others? Did she not know that this would put them in danger? This question haunts me! Maybe, I do not want the answer.

After many hours of revelation and discussion, we (three) children decided to confront our father. We arrived early the next morning; he and our mother were sitting at the kitchen table appearing to be waiting for us. He admitted to the most recent allegations of molestation and to molesting children that had been in my mother's care over the years. Since he was "on a roll," so to speak, I thought the time had finally come to hear him admit his molestation of me. There had been times over the past few years when my father had been ill and thought to be dying; I had sat next to what I thought was his deathbed, while waiting for him to say that he was sorry. I thought that he might want to relieve himself of his guilt before he met his "Maker." Nary a word was said. Perhaps he felt no feelings of guilt. As I stood in the kitchen that day I naively thought this day could be different. I believed at that moment, I still had not only the ability to forgive, but also to work toward repairing the relationship. I wanted my parents to be my parents. After him telling us that the devil was in him, but God had forgiven him, I looked at him (straight in the eyes) asking if there were things that he needed to say about what he had done to me when I was young. With stone cold eyes, he said to me "I have no idea what you're talking about." I only thought myself capable of violence on a few occasions in my life; this was definitely one of them. My swing was fortunately deflected by my one of my brothers. I am very glad (now) that my fist did not connect to his face. Though, in that moment he inflicted the greatest amount of pain ever, at the end of the table with her head hung, sat my mother; drinking her coffee. She may as well have been watching old movies again. By now, there had been at least two allegations and she had still allowed him to be alone with young girls, even family members! I pray that no one else takes the chance with their children in trusting her again. As I write this, the only emotion that I can feel for her is pity. She is still with my father, even after his later confession (not to me, of course) that I had been one of his long-term victims. As a mother myself, I cannot understand why she allowed this to happen to all of the others and me? No one, probably not even him, knows how many victims there have been (the average molester has 115 victims before they are caught). What possible reason would she have to stay when other options, were made available to her? In my opinion, she is just as guilty as he is! Justice does occur, but not always in this lifetime!

As per our demands, our father turned himself into the police and admitted to the latest molestation. I, finally, felt justice would occur; he would be punished and no one else would be hurt. I offered my help to the County Prosecutors Office. I was asked to come in and make a statement. I was very open about the abuse that I had suffered. I talked about my mother having in-home childcare for twenty years and asked if this combination was common in molestation cases. I suggested that interviewing some of the now grown potential victims, between the ages of twenty and forty-five, may shed some light on my father's past. They seemed very interested while thanking me for the information. While I was there, I found out that one of my cousins, age twenty, had been in to report that my father had molested her while under my mother's care just six years ago. When I got home I called her. I felt the need to apologize to her; again my guilt! If I had only told more people, spoke up sooner, and screamed louder. At least, this case should still be prosecuted as I read the law.

My guilt for "not doing more" forced me to do all I could to try to get my father off the street in order that he could not hurt anyone else. I was accused of seeking revenge. Trust me, if I truly wanted revenge, my actions would have included more creativity and pain. Every two to three weeks, I would call the Prosecutors Office to see if there was any more that I could do. I even offered to do some of the investigative work to find and talk to possible victims. I was told these people were adults (now) and it would be difficult to track them down. I had a sinking feeling in the pit of my stomach, though I tried to stay positive. I know county offices are over-worked, so, right or wrong, I decided to do some investigating myself. It had been twenty-five years since I had much contact with that community, but I remembered a few people. I started making phone calls and within three days I found seven more victims; six of whom never had told anyone what happened to them. They all suffered from similar physical and emotional problems as mine and they had experienced numerous relationship problems. All but one, said they would talk to the Prosecutors office "if" called upon, but voluntarily offering information would be too difficult. I was excited. If I could find seven victims in three days, imagine what a professional could do! I was sure there would be more, some probably very recent. I passed my new information on to the Prosecutor's Office; ridiculously thinking they might find it helpful. I was told "if" these women would come in the Prosecutors might find time to talk to them. I tried to explain their fears; the stigma of reporting as opposed to answering questions. The guilt and shame these women carried was paralyzing. This seemed to be ignored and it was becoming clear to me that a forty-year pedophile would most likely remain free in the community. Emotionally, I tried to regroup. In a few weeks, I called again to find out if I would be able to testify at the sentencing hearing. This time the Prosecutor, himself told me to leave him alone and furthermore, he had no interest in investigating the case any further. His comment to me inferred I was the only one who cared about the case. Although dejected, I felt strongly it was my duty to help prevent future victims; I could not let it go! I got wind of a plea-bargain which would not even get my father, an admitted pedophile, very little time off the street. We were eleven months from the time of his admission and arrest, and he had not spent one night in jail nor had the nature of his arrest been in the local paper. I continued to make phone calls to other county officials in order to get someone to understand the seriousness of this case. The county sheriff, the arresting officer, had been my softball coach in high school, therefore I decided to try talking to him. After hearing all of the above details, he was enraged. He had no idea of any other possible related circumstances. He said he wanted to expand the investigation and told me how bad he felt he had not recognized the symptoms of my abuse in order to help me years ago. I assured him that I was very well trained to hide them and it was not his fault. Within the hour, a State Police Sexual Crimes Investigator called me; we talked extensively. He said he was going to re-open and expand this investigation. I gave him the information I had gathered and a few other leads of names I had remembered. He seemed grateful, I felt hope.

On Thursday, December14th, 2000 I called the Prosecutor's Office to confirm the date of my father's hearing. I was told I needed to speak to the Prosecutor directly and that he would call me back. Within two hours, he called, sounding as though he was very angry with me. He told me if I wanted to know anything about this case I could drive to the courthouse to find out. I lived two hours away. He also stated he heard that I had been slandering him and accusing him of neglecting his job. Evidently, the sexual crimes investigator had been asking questions. I told him I just wanted everything possible to be done to protect the community. **His next comment to me was that if anyone was to blame for these so-called victims, it was I, for not telling when I was a child.** Hearing this from the man who was suppose to be prosecuting my father was devastating to me.

As a survivor, I knew, intellectually, he was wrong! However, as a recovering victim my pain, guilt, shame and suffering reached an all time high. I felt threatened, harassed and degraded by this prosecutor. I thought the prosecution was supposed to represent the victims.

The sentencing hearing was "finally" scheduled to take place in April, 2001. Since his arrest fifteen months prior, my father has been continuing his life in the community. Nothing has appeared in the local paper regarding his arrest or guilty plea. Months before I had called the Editor to report the story and commented that in my community a story appears at the time of the arrest. At least, this would make people aware so they would be careful with their own children. She did not know why this particular story had not appeared in the paper, but she would look into it. Nothing appeared. How many more were molested during those fifteen months?

I was informed by other family members that his plea bargain was to be: one year work release, one year home-detention and two years probation. I was in shock! **This punishment does not fit the crime! Not even for one of us, not even for the pain and shame we suffer on any good day of our lives.** However, I came up with an idea. I knew the judge did not have to sign the agreement and he could sentence him to at least four years in prison, even though that would not be enough, it was better than the former. Since none of the past victims, including myself, were going to be allowed to speak, all I had to do was to get my father to ask to speak in open court before the sentencing and admit everything. I know this tactic sounds laughable considering the power and domination that he has had over me all of my life, but through the process, I have developed strength and boldness that I did not know

I had. One week before the hearing I called my father; not sure exactly what I was going to say. He answered, and recognizing my voice started talking quickly, telling me that he was taking his punishment and God had forgiven him of all his sins and now I should do the same. I told him that my forgiveness was between me and God, but that I thought his being forgiven may have something to do with confessing before man. And going into a court of law with his high- powered attorney and getting the least amount of punishment he could receive did not sound to me like someone who was taking his punishment. I told him I might feel a duty, when this was all over, to sue him in a civil court. I told him I thought that I could probably take everything he owned, not really wanting it, but to support the other victims who could not afford their own therapy. Since confession was the only way, and it was what he needed; he agreed.

When the day arrived, he did ask to speak in open court against his attorney's advice, where he admitted to forty plus years of molesting. He admitted to molesting me, other relatives, and numerous other children. He said he was very sorry, and for a moment I felt hope for his soul. Then he said **"but your Honor, I did not know that I was doing anything wrong."** I remembered him telling me as a child not to tell our secret or Daddy would get into trouble. I felt as though there was no air in the room. I wanted to run out and breathe, but I needed to hear and see what would happen and the action of the judge. The judge, looking confused, asked the prosecutor if he had any problem with this plea agreement, the prosecutor said that he was fine with it, therefore the judge signed the agreement. The gavel went down and everyone walked out.

I believe I remained in shock for a week, although I continued to function. My mind kept returning to those early years of physical, emotional and sexual abuse. More of my memories have become clear, but I still have big pockets of time which are gone. I never seem to remember leaving his room. I will recall the pornography, his erection, telling me to take off all of my underwear because there were some new things that he needed to teach me. Then I draw a blank. I do not remember my father having intercourse with me, but I cannot say that he did not. What is sadder is the realization I am not sure I would feel any different one way or the other. The actions to others and me were not only robbing us of our innocence, but he awakened our sexuality well before it was time. He ripped a huge hole into mine and others' lives. I have years of education, training, and have regularly received the help I need, and years have passed, I recognize a part of me is still missing. It is like an illness that will never completely heal. Now, at age forty-eight, I am partially disabled, with a wheel chair in my trunk, which I desperately try not to need.

This revelation brings me to the health problems I believe are a direct result of the trauma of my past. My symptoms started in my early twenties with migraine headaches, muscle pain, joint pain, fatigue, and neck and shoulder pain which never goes away. I also have gastrointestinal problems, panic disorder, depression, asthma and more. I have seen many doctors over the years. I think most of them thought me to be a hypochondriac, but I knew the symptoms were getting worse. I have had approximately fourteen surgeries, I guess the doctors thought taking things out would help, but my symptoms only progressed. Five years ago, I was exasperated with my health and with doctors.

By 1998, I knew my health was going downhill fast. There had to be a reason! I could not feel this bad everyday, and still keep working and smiling on the outside. After an extensive search, I found a doctor who actually took the time to listen to what I wanted to say and explain all of my symptoms. Within minutes, the total symptoms made sense to her giving me the diagnosis of **fibromyalgia.** I felt relieved. It had a name! But what is the prognosis, what is the treatment and how did I get it? Since I had gone twenty years without treatment, the prognosis was not good. The treatment involves a great deal of medication and painful physical therapy. Moreover, how did I get it? She told me the medical community was not exactly sure, but most generally there had been some kind of trauma. I left the doctor's office relieved, but thinking she meant some kind of "physical" trauma which could be the cause of my twenty years of pain and agony. Therefore, I did more research and consulted with a neurologist. She confirmed my Fibromyalgia, but after going without treatment as long as I had, our only goal would be to minimize the pain as much as possible and continue working as long as I could. She also said my stage of Fibromyalgia was as if I had a terminal illness, "only" you do not get to die. Now, the real "kicker," my research revealed the trauma my doctor talked about could be "emotional" trauma, **so the root of all my years of pain and suffering, as well as my depression, and anxiety disorders were most likely due to my sexual abuse.** Imagine; finding out that the "hell" you experienced growing up now has manifested physically, and you get to live with it forever! **What was my shame, as a child, is now my pain as an adult.** Every day when I get up, where my first steps feel as though I am walking on nails, my back and neck in agony, I am reminded of my father. His selfish need to fulfill his sick sexual desires has changed the course of my life forever. If not for my faith in God and the knowledge that He can use anything for His glory, the devotion and love of my husband, the love and help from my sons and daughters-in-law, I am not sure, nor do I believe I could go on.

Each and every day my physical and emotional pain becomes a catalyst for me in having more empathy for people; no matter what they have experienced. I know that I am a different person because of my past, but I know that it is my choice to use those experiences to help others. As long as my body and mind will allow, I will continue to help others. I need to stay aware of how the past still affects my reactions and my feelings. The pain and suffering does not stop with me; my husband and sons have experienced effects as well. They, in turn, effect those close to them. This creates a "ripple effect" and this is just from my abuse. When the abuse of all the others effected by my father is considered, the "ripples" become waves.

I have asked my husband to express his feelings. Instead of me trying to explain how he has felt or, how his life has been altered, I have asked him to not worry about how the truth may hurt me, but to express his feelings" (Eve, 2004).

## Husband:

"Memories or dreams? Were the thoughts of my new bride real? There was confusion on both our parts. Neither one of us wanted to believe these thoughts. But, they kept coming. Anger, rage, vengeance? These were the feelings I felt even before I knew the thoughts were real. Being a very protective person, I wanted to right the wrongs and take the punitive measures into my own hands. My wife was not believed by her own family and had "separated" due to "past situations." Her own brothers were aware of some improprieties, but would not face them nor dare ask. I soon realized that my wife tried to cope with feelings of inferiority by becoming the "hero," the do-it-all, to be the best at everything. Psychologically, this was an attempt to cope with the past. Shopping may now be an alternative to low levels of neuro-chemical imbalances. Rarely can she buy clothes for herself. My parents thought she was "manipulative" and have still never fully understood her past and present pain. She withdrew from my anger even when it was not directed at her. Anger was a trigger that would put her in an "emotional shell." She would rarely get involved in times of others' anger. She had seen me explode even in righteous anger and had told me she had second thoughts of our getting married prior to marriage. Later, she told me the consequences of her parents' anger toward her although she might not be the cause. It is so rare when I can choose to watch an old movie. Old movies were what my mother-in-law would watch downstairs while her daughter was sent up to satisfy the Pedophile. There are still some wholesome, old movies that I feel I cannot watch because it will trigger an anxiety attack or at least bad memories. I feel I must at least announce from a distance that I am watching something of which she would not be reminded. Get cold at bedtime? I don't dare mention a TV commercial regarding electric blankets! One of her worst memories was getting caught under the electric blanket with her father, BY HER MOTHER! I just try to remember and turn up the heat to avoid another lecture about past injustices. One of our worst times of communication was just two weeks ago by my forgetting. You could say it has affected our relationship and marriage. This came after twenty-seven years of marriage. Both of our adult sons have expressed their feelings to the perpetrator - their grandfather! I am still surprised that they have not expressed their feelings physically! How has her health affected our marriage? She was once the "Susie-homemaker," cooking, cleaning, mowing, gardening, and raising children. The boys are now gone, but a housecleaner has been hired. The survivor awaits opportunities in which others can do her wishes – she can no longer physically manage a household or entertain guests without help. Her frustration at losing her former self, maybe, is now accepted. She has mostly given up driving due to her slow reaction time. She "feels like an invalid." The result is that I have become the "caretaker." I must cook, clean, assist with venturing to the kitchen, assisting to the bathroom when fibro takes over, or run errands. Handling a wheel chair for daily walks and shopping. I do get my exercise, but not by playing. She struggles to get weekly exercise – what will be the impact of her poor health on her lifespan? This was not the future I would have predicted for middle-aged parents who were used to physical activity and sports. The pain doesn't go away – everyone connected has to deal with this past. Revenge? How about kicking the pedophile in the groin every week for the rest of his life, so that the bastard can realize the pain he has caused families – his own, his extended family, and families of neighbors and strangers. Justice??? Not enough! One year of work release, one year of home-detention, followed by two years of probation – he got away with murder – the killing of people's feelings and emotions. Everyone whom he has touched physically or emotionally has been affected negatively!! "The ripples continue."

Eve:

"I pray my story be heard so that my father or any other molester does not have the opportunity to take away the innocence, safety, trust, self-esteem and dignity of one more child and other victims get the courage to speak up. Our silence only perpetuates more abuse. I beg families to stop hushing and covering up this type of behavior and the legal system will treat these crimes against children with more than an insignificant slap on the wrist. When they get off so easy, our suffering is invalidated. "We" the victims carry this pain and shame our entire lives. **I, for one, refuse to remain silent any longer!** To the best of my recollection the above account is true" (Eve, 2004).

This is the life of one woman who has become not only a survivor, but a support for others moving from the role of victim to survivor. Becoming a survivor is a process, and not an easy one. For this woman, the key to her recovery is helping others as well as disconnecting from her perpetrator. Most women are not able to put the abuse behind them because they keep their abusers in their lives. Some even allow their abusing parents to care for their own children. Why, with the knowledge they have, would they even consider putting their own children in danger? Denial is a safe option – temporarily. The emphasis here is on the word temporary. Secrets, like prejudice, are very carefully taught. However, when the secrets are exposed, chaos unfolds. As can be seen from the study of Eve's life, revealing secrets brought her ridicule, blame and isolation. Fortunately, she found her solace spiritually and from her newly created family. Her healing continues each day as she aides in the healing of others.

The "ripple effect" of this case is evident through the lives of all those touched by it. Eve has turned her experiences into a positive "ripple" through the lives of those she affects. Another positive "ripple" is her own family's healthy relationships, largely due to her consciously choosing to change the course of her family tree. However, most of the "ripples" for Eve and her father's other victims are extremely negative and many other repercussions are yet to come.

# CHAPTER 3

## DEFINITIONS AND CHARACTERISTICS OF CHILDHOOD SEXUAL ABUSE

### DEFINITIONS:

A discussion of definitions, statistics and prevalence in child abuse give rise to unavoidable controversies and biases. The term abuse suggests that a wrong has been perpetrated upon someone. The definition of abuse varies somewhat from culture to culture. The definition of sexual abuse has been particularly unclear due to the reticence of most societies to discuss human sexuality and sexual matters openly. This reticence has been aptly described as follows:

> 'Sexual expression as any other than in the missionary position,' between a 'man and wife' for the purpose of producing children, was once an offence against canon law, and a sin in the eyes of the Christian Church... in 1976, masturbation was a sin, and in the nineteenth century, there was a flourishing trade in mechanical restraints to prevent children from playing with their genitals (Silverman, 2002).

In today's culture, these restraints could be considered a form of sexual abuse. There was also a time, not so long ago, when rape was not recognized within a marriage, sex was expected upon demand, and sex or sexual exploration, of any kind, was acceptable within a family. For most families, sex is an inappropriate topic of discussion even though the act may be expected (Russell, 1986). The continual perpetration of this ignorant style of living leaves children ill-equipped to discern whether or not an authority figure has their best interests at heart.

In order for a child to be repeatedly abused, as in the families of incest, the child would have to be convinced to believe that what is happening to him or her is absolutely normal. In order to normalize an abnormal situation, a specific set of lies must be taught:

1) Abuse is normal. Therefore, your distressing emotional response is wrong and you are bad for having those feelings.

2) Abuse is justified. You have a basic flaw or evil in you that elicits the abuse.

3) Abuse is necessary. You have to tolerate it because it keeps the family together.

4) Being a good child means behaving as if this is a perfect family. Abusive families are deeply invested in maintaining the public image of being perfectly happy and problem free (Wilson, 2001).

With these lies, it is possible for a child to believe their family was and is normal. The possible adverse effects to come for the child may not appear until adulthood. This mental preparation grooms victims then to believe they are not as good as others. They are damaged goods. This plays a major role in their development of self-worth and self-evaluations. Although, most child sexual abuse does not involve violence, it does involve coercion. The relationship developed between the victim and the perpetrator is based upon a misrepresentation as to what constitutes normal, and the child is manipulated by the imbalance of power. The victim is usually dependent upon the perpetrator, thus feeling that they must do what is asked and keep the secret, thus representing what they have been taught as normal (Courtois, 1988). Also, most children are taught from a young age to obey adults who are in a position of authority. This simple teaching, as respectful as it may seem, could set up a child as prime pickings for a seasoned pedophile.

## LEGAL DEFINITIONS

Sexual abuse is broadly defined as any type of sexual activity with a child that involves either force or coercion, or that occurs between the child and someone much older. Specific laws regarding the age at which someone can consent to sexual contact with an adult varies by state. Usually, the age of consent is between 14 and 18 years of age. Sexual activity includes both sexual contact as well as noncontact sexual experiences, such as being exposed to pornography or exhibitionism (Naugle, 2004).

Another definition of sexual abuse is the adult contact of a child for that adult's stimulation. The abuser is typically older and in a position of authority over that child. Sexual abuse also includes persuasion, inducement, excitement, or coercion of a child, basically, any form of sexual exploitation of children (Sagatun, Edwards, 1995).

Bass and Davis (1988) defined childhood sexual abuse as an interaction between an adult and child that includes any and/or all of the following: (1) touching or asking a child to touch the adult's or the child's genitals, (2) fondling, (3) kissing, (4) rubbing, (5) rape, (6) intrusive looks, (7) oral sex, (8) anal sex, (9) extensive nudity, (10) incest, (11) child pornography, (12) subjecting child to pornography, (13) encouraging sexual play, and (14) sexual torture.

## DEFINITIONS OF INCEST

Incest is not easily defined. The legal definition and the psychological definition differ considerably. The legal definition is very simple and narrow. It is described as sexual intercourse between blood relatives. Due to this narrow definition, many people have been confused as to what happened to them as children. If penetration had not occurred, incest had not occurred. Incest, from a psychological view point, covers a much wider range of relationships and behaviors. These include all of the above listed interactions between child and adult where the adult is sexually stimulated, in a position of power and is or is thought to be a member of the family. Penetration is not necessary for the child to be violated and damaged. The secretive nature of the act is also indicative of sexual abuse (Forward, 1989).

> A father who affectionately hugs and kisses his child is doing nothing that needs to be kept secret. In fact, such touching is essential to a child's wellbeing. But if that father strokes the child's genitals or makes the child stroke his; that is an act that must be kept secret. This is an act of incest (Forward, 1989).

Psychological incest can also include subtle behaviors. Just having one's privacy invaded, as in being spied upon while dressing or bathing, is abusive. Even if a behavior does not fit the literal definition of incest, if the child feels violated, he or she may suffer the same psychological damage as those actually penetrated (Forward, 1989).

## CHARACTERISTICS:

First, are the signs of sexual abuse easy to read? The signs can sometimes be impossible to notice or as they were posted on a billboard. Regardless, the signs are there. In our case study, Eve was very careful to keep the secret while she was a child. Those who knew Eve well during her childhood have commented on how they should have known, but she always seemed so happy. Eve exhibited the extreme of extraversion; she worked very hard to prove that she and her family were normal. When she left her home in the morning she put on her face, the face that she wanted the world to see. Eve was involved in everything the school had to offer: cheerleading, yearbook staff, softball, chess, and drama. Drama was her favorite, she did not have to be herself, she could take on the identity of someone else. She could be anyone else, just not herself.

The other end of the extreme is the introvert. They are quiet, withdrawn, shy and usually alone. These symptoms are sometimes easier for a professional to identify. These children show there is probably something wrong in their home.

But a child victimized by abuse and needing to express these pains is put in a double bind: if they choose to survive by acting out their anger in various delinquent activities, they are discounted and discredited for causing further problems, and if they attempt to hide their pain and shame under a serene exterior, they are seen as not having suffered any real harm (Ebby, 2004).

## Red flags to watch for with young children:

A child putting his or her mouth on another's sexual parts
A child asking to engage in sexual acts
A child masturbating with an object
A child inserting an object into his or her own anus or vagina
A child imitating intercourse
A child imitating sexual sounds
French kissing by a child
A child talking about explicit sexual acts
A child undressing others
A child asking to watch explicit sexual television or movies
A child using sexual words
A child imitating sexual acts with dolls

## Signs of sexual abuse in children:

crying, bedwetting, withdrawing, regressive behavior, concentration problems, self-abuse, acting out sexually, difficulty walking or sitting, irritation of mouth, irritation of genitals, refusal to go certain places, destructive behaviors, running away, nightmares, physical illness, headaches, fear of a specific adult, using sexual words beyond child's knowledge, torn stained or bloody underclothing

## Signs of Sexual Abuse in Teenagers:

depression, withdrawing, running away, alcohol/drug abuse, eating disorders, self-injury, suicide attempts, poor self-image, prostitution, acting out behavior, recurrent physical complaints, school problems, lying, negative attitude and fear of sex, poor peer relationships, promiscuity, overly seductive behaviors (APRI, 2004).

"There are a wide range of potential adverse outcomes associated with childhood sexual abuse. However, there is no unique pattern to these long term effects and no discernable specific post-abuse syndrome" (Mullen, Martin, Anderson, Romans, & Herbison, 1996). The effects range from nothing of any significance to extreme psychological dysfunction. The most extreme cases are those children who, in order to survive both physically and emotionally, are those who learn to deny their emotions. In his 2003 writing, Lev describes the feeling of horror in their lives – that there is no way out, normal functioning is impossible, and these children learn to block out as much as they can for as long as they can (Lev, 2003). Blocking trauma is a common defense mechanism by children, one that is effective in childhood, but often destructive in adult life. Children are not the only ones who deny the abuse. The spouse of the abuser, the parents who do not want to accept reality or any one close to the victim who does not want to deal with what has happened can be said to deny the abuse.

Alfred Adler, noted psychological theorist, says that one's view of self in relation to the world and the ability to socialize is developed at a young age and that perception continues through adulthood (Adler, 1956). As young children, the world revolves around parents, and the child's sense of normalcy is developed. If the sense of normalcy is sexual abuse, then this view serves to develop a child's place and function in the world. If this sense of normalcy continues, what kind of parent will a child become or what kind of relationships will he or she develop? If this permeates the adult self and becomes their "normal" way of living, they not only give their abusive parents their childhood innocence, but their whole lives as well. For the child to normalize abuse, he or she must take on the blame for that abuse, therefore leading to guilt and a very low sense of self worth.

According to Susan Forward (1989), children suffering from all forms of abuse, including incest, internalize blame. The major difference with incest victims is that the blame is compounded by the shame. These children vehemently believe that the incest was their fault entirely. This belief intensifies strong feelings of self-loathing as well as shame. While they are trying to cope with actual incest, these children feel compelled to guard against being caught and being exposed. They feel dirty and disgusting. These feelings are manifested in adulthood with feelings of being hopelessly inadequate. They also deal with feelings of being worthless and genuinely bad. Adult survivors of childhood sexual abuse share a legacy of tragic feelings, referred to by Forward (1989) as the Three D's of incest: Dirty, Damaged, and Different.

Taking one's parents off the pedestal helps the victim to understand that his or her denial of how abusive his or her parents were has allowed them to pretend he or she has the perfect family. Bass and Davis (1988) describe several coping mechanisms used by survivors. These include the following: (1) denial, (2) rationalizing, (3) creating chaos, (4) repeating abuse, (5) compulsive eating, (6) fantasizing, (7) perfectionism, (8) self-mutilation, (9) compulsive exercising, (10) shoplifting, (11) abusing others, (12) avoiding intimacy, (13) creating new personalities, (14) forgetting, (15) leaving your body, (16) staying in control, (17) gambling, (18) minimizing, (19) staying busy, (20) alcoholism, (21) anorexia/bulimia, (22) workaholism, (23) taking care of others, (24) hiding behind a partner, (25) sleeping excessively, (26) humor,

(27) not sleeping, (28) dogmatic beliefs, (29) running away, (30) suicide attempts, (31) drug addiction, (32) compulsive sex, (33) avoiding sex, (34) spacing out, and (35) staying super alert.

Of the children who report little to no effects and those who report "rising above" the abuse, a commonality exists. These survivors seem to have had high levels of (non-abusive) parental support, strong support from peers, pre-existing high levels of self-esteem and good intellectual skills (Bagley, Mallick, 1999).

# Chapter 4
## THE PERPETRATOR

An adult, age sixteen or over who is at least five years older than the child, and who perpetrates some form of sexual activity upon a prepubescent child, generally age thirteen years or younger, is a child molester (Socarides & Loeb, 2004). "Currently, there is no psychological or behavioral profile that fits all adult sexual abusers" (Schlesinger, 2000).

Pedophiles generally report an attraction to children of a specific age range and sex. Some pedophiles are attracted only to children; others are occasionally attracted to adults as well.

> Pedophiles who act on their urges with children may limit their activity to undressing the child and looking, exposing themselves, masturbating in the presence of the child, or gentle touching and fondling of the child. Others, however, perform fellatio or cunnilingus on the child or penetrate the child's vagina, mouth, or anus with their fingers, foreign objects, or penis and use varying degrees of force to do so. These activities are commonly explained with excuses or rationalizations that they have "educational value" for the child, that the child derives "sexual pleasure" from them, or that

the child was "sexually provocative..." (DSM-IV-TR, 2000, pp. 571).

Pedophiles can be very smooth and manipulative. They can exhibit great patience while convincing other professionals of their normalcy. With their victims, they will sometimes spend months in the "grooming" process. Grooming is preparing a child for meeting the pedophile's sexual needs, getting the child to think that they love them more than anyone else, and understand them better than anyone else. Pedophiles must also take great care in normalizing all steps of sexual encounters so that the child will think them normal and so that the two of them develop a great bond and the secret remains just between the two of them (Bass & Davis, 1988). "Once the abusive relationship is established, the offender uses many techniques to maintain it. These may include giving gifts and the appeal of keeping secrets, as well as bribery, threats, and physical aggression" (Schlesinger, 2000).

A child sex offender is an adult who uses children, in any way, for his or her own sexual pleasure. This can include touching, asking a child to touch, fondling, kissing as an adult would kiss, rubbing, intrusive looks, showing the child adult pornography, oral or anal sex, exposing the child to their nudity, having the child take their clothes off, incest, taking nude pictures of the child, and/or encouraging the child to act in a sexual way.

Unfortunately, sex offenders do not have a specific profile. Even so, some observations can be made. Abusers are most generally in a position of authority. They have power, trust, or control over their victims. These perpetrators usually appear normal and intelligent. They provide for their families financially and are active in their communities. And, oddly enough, they have no prior criminal history (APRI, 2004).

Perhaps the true definition can come only from child molesters themselves. Although, trusting the validity of their answers is difficult. In *The Mind of the Pedophile*, edited by Socarides and Loeb, the thoughts of pedophiles are studied in order to understand their minds and thought processes. They have concluded there is not just one type of pedophile, but pedophilias. This is a group of conditions with similar sexual aims – sexual relations with prepubescent children – but with different causative processes and different levels of fixation, resulting in various degrees of severity and different prognoses for recovery" (Socarides & Loeb, 2004). In this work, Socarides (2004) separates the classifications on the basis of diagnosis: obligatory, variational, situational, oedipal, and/or pre-oedipal, and those that involve schizophrenia.

> The situational and variational forms of pedophilia are considered non-clinical forms of sexual perversion. The former is characterized by (1) environmental inaccessibility to adult partners of the opposite sex; (2) consciously motivated behavior; (3) pedophile acts that are not fear-induced but arise out of conscious deliberation and choice; (4) the inability to function with an adult partner of the opposite sex; and (5) a flexible sexual pattern that allows individuals to return to adult opposite-sex partners when they are available (Socarides & Loeb, 2004).

As the subtitle suggests, variational pedophilia is as varied as the dependency sought by men and women or entirely the product of individual enterprise. It can be implied from this work that these forms of pedophilia are not considered clinical because the perpetrator is able to return to a functional relationship with an adult member of the opposite sex. "Latent forms of this perversion may erupt into oedipal, pre-oedipal, or schizo-pedophilia" (Socarides & Loeb, 2004). Regardless of the number of children that these "non-clinical" pedophiles may have perpetrated, until they reach the latent forms, they seldom present for treatment. Before a diagnosis has been made or a category of pedophilia has been determined, the statement made by an overwhelming number of confronted child molesters is: "I did not know I was doing any thing wrong." In any form of treatment for a repeated or addictive behavior, such as alcoholism, drug abuse, gambling, pornography or the above perversion, accepting that one has done something wrong is the psychological basis for treatment. The degree to which a behavior is considered socially acceptable affects the degree of denial that must be overcome in treatment. Other than an individual suffering from an extreme mental illness, one who has decided that there is nothing wrong with the molestation of a child has either normalized a trauma involving molestation from his or her own past or he or she is narcissistic in nature and feels sexually inadequate with his or her peers.

Although it is difficult to determine how an individual becomes a pedophile, there are three specific areas where pedophiles differ from the norm, or "normal" individual. The first has to do with empathy or the lack thereof. These offenders seem to completely disregard and invade the privacy of their victims. Empathic skills requires one to identify with the emotions of another. In pedophiles, this skill seems to be nonexistent. By not empathizing with the victim, the pedophile can normalize her offenses. There seems to be nothing in her mind to tell her what she is doing is wrong or harmful to the child. Pedophiles also have difficulty maintaining social relationships with their peers. Good socialization skills involve some degree of good decision-making and the ability to successfully process emotions. Again, the pedophile lacks these skills. Third, pedophiles seems void of negative consequential feelings, so they may continue their predatory nature without the cognition of guilt (Geer, J., Estupinan,M. & Manguno-Mire, G. 1999).

As per the definitions, the illustrative case study of Eve indicates that she was definitely a victim of incest and that her father was not just an opportunist with his own daughter. He included many others for his sexual fulfillment and seemed to have some specific age preferences. He, by definition, is a pedophile.

## ARE PEDOPHILES TREATABLE?

If, in fact, the pedophile can be treated, this treatment must come from a therapist who specializes in this field. The major objective in treatment is to reduce the probability of recidivism or re-offending.

In order to treat any psychological disorder a professional needs to have some working knowledge of the disorder and its origin. How does a pedophile become a pedophile? An answer to this question proved illusive. Douglas and Olshaker (1997) discuss the inherent problems of the treatment of pedophiles. The problems of treatment lie mutually in the mental health profession and the law enforcement world. "The mental health discipline is unsure of how and why individuals build this sexual desire for children, and thus, there is an etiological problem" (Douglas & Olshaker, 1997). In *The Outpatient Treatment of Child Molesters*, Stan Friedman (1991) recognizes the idea that the offender is never cured. This program encourages graduates of the program to remain with a counselor or with a group for self-monitoring (Friedman, 1991). If even those who treat molesters are unsure of their recovery, what must we deduce from this? Given this and the fact that most child sexual abuse is never brought to the attention of the authorities, our hopes for treatment decline.

Another fact to ponder regarding pedophile recovery is "Meagan's Law." Since 1996 child sex offenders have been required to register their whereabouts with local authorities every time they move. They must do this for the rest of their lives and this information is made accessible to the public. Is this required of any other crime? This requirement says much for how our society feels about pedophile recovery. However, does this just tell parents to be aware of where convicted molesters live and to watch their children? Perhaps, this is a feeble attempt to show society the perceived seriousness of the crime, when actually it puts the offenders back on the street and out of prison and places responsibility for the reduction in crime in the hands of innocent families.

As stated above, the major objective in treatment is to reduce the probability of recidivism, however, in order to test the treatment, the reintroduction of the sexual offender back into the general population must occur. Recidivism tells us the percentage of offenders who re-offend. Given the previously quoted number (115) of how many victims a child sex offender has abused before he suffers legal consequences, how can we even hope to presume that the now treated and "educated" pedophile will not be exceptionally better at his game and more skilled at avoiding legal consequences? Though testing exists, even those who specialize in the field are not completely trusting of psychological testing as a means to determine if an offender may return to society.

I believe we have established that the only way to find out if a child molester is treatable is to allow her to be around children again. If the information were available, would The Society of Prevention of Cruelty to Animals ever consider it humane to allow someone who has abused a dog (to the point of lifelong damage) to adopt a dog from the local shelter? If the answer to this question is no, then why should random children be used as lab rats in order to test the validity of some professional's theory on child molesters? These are questions to ponder. It would appear, the only way to determine if a pedophile is treatable is to put children at risk.

# CHAPTER 5

## IMPACTS OF CHILDHOOD SEXUAL ABUSE

In times of strife, an old phrase is commonly used: "at least you have your health." Usually, this phrase is used by individuals who have not experienced extreme pain or loss in their personal life. When we hear of a child that has been molested, similar comments are made, such as, "at least she was not penetrated," "at least she's not pregnant," or "surely she is too young to remember." These phrases, whether intended or not, invalidate the feelings of a victim. This invalidation as to the damage done, regardless of the manner in which the molestation occurred, causes some victims to sink further and further into their sickness. It is a sickness to cover up and keep the family's dirty secrets hidden deep inside. It is like having an open wound, one that has salt poured on it from time to time.

Mental health issues can be broken down, simply, into two categories: those inherited from family genes and those brought on by emotional or physical traumas (Corsini & Wedding, 2005). The symptoms, however, can be interpreted similarly. For the purpose of this project, the mental health issues brought on by trauma will be discussed.

## PSYCHIATRIC SYMPTOMS ASSOCIATED WITH CHILD ABUSE:

> Symptoms of Post Traumatic Stress Disorder include; nightmares, flashbacks, memory and concentration problems, hyperarousal, hypervigilance, intrusive memories, avoidance, abnormal startle response and feeling worse when reminded of trauma.
>
> Dissociative Disorders include; out of body experiences, derealization, amnesia, a fragmented sense of self and identity,
>
> Anxiety issues include; panic attacks, claustrophobia, substance abuse, alcoholism and drug addiction (Bremner, 1997).

Personality disorders have been linked to childhood sexual abuse, one particular diagnosis is Borderline Personality Disorder. This diagnosis will be discussed later in this chapter.

According to Bremner (1997), one of the most common diagnoses associated with childhood sexual abuse is Post Traumatic Stress Disorder (PTSD). In addition, according to Foe, Keane & Friedman (2000), with the psychological symptoms of fear, anxiety and concentration problems, there is a physiological component dealing with the hippocampal area of the brain. This will be discussed, in detail, in the next section of this project.

> PTSD is a serious psychological condition that occurs as a result of experiencing a traumatic event. The symptoms that characterize PTSD are reliving the traumatic event or frightening elements of it; avoidance of thoughts, memories, people, and places associated

with the event; emotional numbing, and symptoms of elevated arousal. Often accompanied by other psychological disorders, PTSD is a complex condition that can be associated with significant morbidity, disability, and impairment of life functions (Foa, Keane & Friedman, 2000).

PTSD is not just remembering the traumatic event from the past, but actually feeling as though one is reliving the moment of trauma. Those who suffer from PTSD usually have particular events, sounds, people, places, things, smells and more that trigger these feelings of reliving the original trauma. This is a difficult concept for one to understand if they have not experienced PTSD. The identification of triggers is a long and arduous process, one that should be facilitated by a therapist. Panic attacks are the most common identifiable symptom of PTSD. When a survivor of childhood sexual abuse experiences a trigger, the ensuing panic attack will probably be his or her first indication that a trigger has been experienced. The survivor may not know why they are exhibiting panic symptoms. However, as they learn, through the counseling process, to recognize the triggers, they will have the tools to stop or at least to slow down an attack. This valuable skill may take years to develop and implement. It will also be necessary for the family and loved ones of the survivor to understand and to recognize the triggers. Although, this may be too much to ask of a spouse, the ability for a healthy relationship and positive future will be at stake.

Along with PTSD, another very common reality for survivors of childhood sexual abuse is depression. This form of depression is not a situational depression, but a clinical form of depression. A patient may not even realize the original root of her depression. Instead, she may remain in denial or with portions of her memory blocked.

Depression is an extremely common expression of suppressed incest conflicts. It may range from a general sense of sadness to nearly total immobilization. A disproportionate number of incest victims, particularly women, allow themselves to become overweight as adults. The weight serves two important purposes for the victim: (1) she imagines that it will keep men away from her, and (2) the body mass creates a false illusion of strength and power. Many victims become terrified when they first begin to lose weight because it makes them feel helpless and vulnerable once again (Forward, 1989).

According to a study published in 1999 in *The American Journal of Psychiatry*, there are notable differences relating to depression between women who had experienced childhood sexual abuse and those who had not. Significantly more patients from the group who had experienced childhood sexual abuse had made suicide attempts during their current depression. These patients also had a previous history of self-injury, self-mutilation and had been dependent on alcohol and other drugs (Gladstone et al. 1999). "They tenaciously pursue sexual behaviors in order to help alleviate their relational pain and make themselves feel good, satisfied and in control" (Schaumburg, 1997).

A history of childhood sexual abuse is also associated with a number of long term difficulties in adult life. Sexual abuse victims may have four times greater risk to have symptoms of major depression than individuals without such a history. Sexually abused individuals are also five times as likely to be diagnosed with an anxiety disorder (Naugle, 2004).

These individuals also report having problems controlling their tempers. They exhibit bouts of extreme outbursts of anger, rage and chronic irritability (Naugle, 2004).

Naugle goes on to say that adult survivors have a much higher rate of dissociative symptoms, higher rates of suicide ideation and suicide attempts, as well as stress reducing self-injurious behaviors, such as cutting or burning themselves (Naugle, 2004). Patients report that when they see the blood flow or the skin turn dark red or blister, they feel a release of pressure. Although, these behaviors may have the immediate effect of transferring their unbearable, emotional pain to a more bearable physical pain, the long-term ramifications of this behavior can be life altering.

> Abstaining from destructive behavior became dependent on dealing with one's past. The main concept of the inner child theory is a personification of this past. It gives individuals a way to relate to their past in a tangible, rather than abstract manner... This allows [one] to experience the part of [them] who felt the pain as well as the part of [them] who could experience the pain (Taylor, 1991).

As adults, these self-mutilators would, most likely, receive a diagnosis of Borderline Personality Disorder. These women live a life that is filled with extreme conflict in their personal lives. They swing from love to hate in an instant. Overwhelmed with the feeling of real or imagined abandonment, these women suffer from a constant instability of self-perception and chronic feelings of emptiness. Impulsivity that is potentially self-damaging is seriously damaging to potential relationships (DSM-IV-TR, 2000).

"... Over the past two decades there has been an increasing acknowledgement that a high percentage of patients who

DEBRA SUSAN PENROD, PH.D.

qualify for a borderline personality disorder diagnosis have also been traumatized through childhood sexual abuse" (Reavey & Warner, 2003).

Although impulsive self-injurious behaviors are often associated with personality disorder diagnoses, people engaging in these behaviors constitute such a large group that it is impossible to make a singular etiological formulation. Typically, impulsive self-injurious behavior is established early in adolescence and often develops into a chronic behavior in adulthood. Impulsive self-injurious behavior can be seen as pathological on one hand and as a self-help strategy on the other hand. Although it is easy to see how self-injurious behavior is destructive, it is also helpful in that it can provide relief from unpleasant experiences and may prevent temporary psychotic episodes and suicidal acts. Research on impulsive self-injurious behavior indicates that it often prevents people from experiencing symptoms such as depersonalization, severe anxiety, intense anger, depression, hallucinations, perceived external or internal flaws, racing thoughts and rapidly fluctuating emotions, boredom and stimulus depravation, and feelings such as loneliness, emptiness, and insecurity. Impulsive self-injurious behavior is often associated with childhood sexual abuse and subsequent PTSD reactions (White, Kress, 2003).

One aspect of self-injurious behavior with a category of its own is Eating Disorders. Although these behaviors are considered mental health issues, they have the potential of becoming physical health issues, and if not treated, physical problems that will lead to death. According to Dr. Stephen Wonderlich (2000), at the University of North Dakota School of Medicine, young girls who are sexually abused are more likely to develop eating disorders. His research is just a sample of the abundance of information suggesting that childhood trauma increases the risk of developing eating disorders. As the dissatisfaction with self grows, a condition known as body dismorphia sets in. Abused girls are more dissatisfied with their bodies and they develop a disorder known as body dismorphia. The image seen in the mirror, by them, is not what is seen by others. Their obsession with weight leads to excessive and extreme dieting (Anorexia Nervosa) or eating and then purging their food by vomiting or using laxatives and diuretics (Bulimia). Abused girls were also more likely to restrict their eating when they were bored or emotionally upset. Wonderlich suggests that the abused might experience higher levels of emotional distress and have trouble coping. Food restriction and perhaps other eating disorder behaviors may reflect efforts to cope with such experiences (Wonderlich, 2000). When the life of a child is out of control, as it is with sexual abuse victims, control is established by eating or not eating. Through this self-destructive behavior, they cope with this feeling of control, albeit a false sense of control.

One of the most serious of the manifestations of destructive behavior and life altering effects of sexual abuse is Dissociative Identity Disorder. Although, this is sometimes difficult to diagnose, it is probably diagnosed too often by professionals who may be a bit over zealous. In order to adequately make this diagnosis, one must uncover the outside layer and look at the core of a person, to their inner child. This inner child holds the memories as well as the keys to healing. The therapist's job is to facilitate the individual in connecting their inner core to their current state.

Dissociation is a mental process, which produces a lack of connection in a person's thoughts, memories, feelings, actions, or sense of identity. During the period of time when a person is dissociating, certain information is not associated with other information as it normally would be. For example, during a traumatic experience, a person may dissociate the memory of the place and circumstances of the trauma from her ongoing memory, resulting in a temporary mental escape from the fear and pain of the trauma and, in some cases, a memory gap surrounding the experience (Sidran Foundation, 2003).

The Dissociative Disorders encompass four basic categories: Dissociative Amnesia, Dissociative Fugue, Dissociative Identity Disorder, and Depersonalization Disorder.

The most common of these diagnoses for childhood sexual abuse survivors is Depersonalization Disorder. Survivors describe times during their childhood when they knew it was time to "go away" or "check out." Some survivors can describe the events leading up to an abusive event, they may even be able to describe part of the event, but then their memories fade to black, so to speak. Some recall a floating sensation and possibly watching from above, others have no recollection of the ending of the event. This might lead one to believe that the ending was too severe for the mind to conceive, so it had no other choice but to fade away. The traumatic event was so overwhelming that there was no physical escape, so the escape had to be mental. Perhaps, there is a place in the brain, a place where bad things do not happen to little girls, a place of peace and comfort where hiding is acceptable. This description sounds a bit like a fairy tale with a happy ending, however, the happy ending does not exist. One may be able to "go away" or depersonalize for a while, but they do come back and what they come back to is no fairy tale. These times (of zoning out) may or may not be remembered later in life, but as discussed earlier, not all memories must be unearthed for one to achieve enough mental stability required for a happy, healthy life.

The most serious of the Dissociative Disorders is Dissociative Identity Disorder (DID), formerly known as Multiple Personality Disorder (APA, 2000). To receive this diagnosis, a patient must exhibit the presence of two or more distinct identities and have these identities or personality states recurrently take control of the individual's behavior. They must have periods of "losing time," having no recollection of things during a specific period of time, and the occurrence of these events is not more accurately explained by alcohol or other drugs (DSM-IV-TR, 2000). There are those who are skeptical about DID, but, perhaps they might understand if they (themselves) had ever experienced an event that was too traumatic to comprehend. These patients go so "far away" that another must take their place, and the other identity could be described as a "fragmented emotion." When working with DID patients, one must be cognizant of the fact that each of these alters may represent a specific emotion and that alter may be the only one capable of that particular emotion. Although the goal is integration, it could take years to reconnect the "fragmented emotions." In addition, the word 'integration' may be a forbidden word during the first few years of treatment. This intricate system of who deals with what event or emotion took an unbearable trauma and years to develop and it has become the defense mechanism for the abused, one that has been effective through childhood and one that is a highly creative coping skill. However, as adults this defensive dissociation can be destructive to family, work, friends, and most daily activities.

One very common longing of a survivor of child sexual abuse is to "make sense" of what has happened to them and to try to understand why. Although this desire is strong, in most cases it does not prove to be a healthy longing. Trying to understand why anyone, especially a parent, would hurt a child in this manner usually leads to confusion, self-degradation, and intense anger.

> One of the aspects of sexual abuse, seen as a post traumatic stress disorder, is a compelling need on the part of the victim/survivor to make sense of the experience, regaining a sense of mastery over the event and enhancing one's self-esteem (Draucker, 1989).

While therapists help their patients come to terms with their past, and help them to accept that not everything has an answer or a reason, it is also important to help them understand that total suppression is not the answer either. Finding a balance may take years of therapy.

> Some therapists have pointed out the danger in the survivor's searching for meaning when there may be none. The ability to block or interrupt thoughts of a negative event may be crucial in living with events that have, in fact, no resolution …the victims of undesirable life events relieved of pain by making conscious attempts to block thoughts of their negative outcomes (Silver, Boon, & Stones, 1983).

## PHYSICAL:

For most, the idea that childhood sexual abuse can cause mental problems is not a great stretch of the imagination. However, understanding the concept that those mental or emotional issues can manifest into actual physical problems is an entirely different way of thinking. The following research should dispel any argument to the contrary.

To a great degree, our physical health has a direct correlation with our mental well-being. As an example, it is commonly known and accepted that stress can be a contributor to many illnesses, such as high blood pressure, strokes, heart problems, and digestive problems, to name a few. Stress is the result of our dealing with everyday problems by internalizing our feelings, feelings that will find a way out, usually in a way that has negative impact on our physical health. Although this is, for the most part, an accepted medical issue, the fact that people with severe trauma in their past could have physical repercussions from that trauma is not so widely accepted or even openly discussed. Could this be another part of the secretive nature of traumas like molestation? Not only do people not want to talk about molestation, but our society does not want to talk about the physical manifestations of that abuse. However, doors are starting to open.

Although millions of children are abused each year, the impact of that abuse from a physiological standpoint is still not widely recognized. The way a child is treated has a great impact on his or her health as an adult.

## THE NEUROENDOCRINE SYSTEM:

The nervous and endocrine system engage in a back and forth dance through which they control the body's physiology by continuously increasing or decreasing the activity of various neurotransmitters and hormones. The brain orchestrates this dance with the goal of maintaining a state of homeostasis or equilibrium. Stressful events disrupt the dance, upsetting its delicate balance. The brain responds by activating the sympathetic nervous system and the hypothalamic-pituitary-adrenal (HPA) axis and releasing endogenous opioids. Stimulation of the sympathetic nervous system results in the release of catecholamines into the blood, while the HPA axis induces the release of glucocorticoids (primarily cortisol). Both catecholamines and cortisol have been found to be chronically elevated in abused children (Putman, Tricket,1997).

Putman and Tricket's article goes on to say that these catecholamine levels rise when stressful events occur. This increased level will result in hypoarousal along with increased heart rate, respiration, blood pressure, and muscle tone. Changes in the central nervous system creates a state of hypervigilance, which leads to the "fight or flight" response. As the levels of catecholamines continue to rise chronically, abnormalities can arise in cardiovascular regulation, along with an increased startle response, profound sleep disturbances, and generalized anxiety (Putman & Trickett, 1997).

Imagine the sexually abused child going to bed each and every night not knowing how or when they will be victimized. The fight or flight response would be a constant thought, and this hypervigilance would become exhausting, making a good deep sleep impossible. Deep sleep is the time for the body to heal itself from the day's activities and injuries. If one's body never heals itself at night as it is programmed to do, how could one even hope for good long-term health? What would happen to muscles that never have a chance to heal themselves? Perhaps, this is a plausible explanation for chronic pain disorders, which is a common complaint of survivors of childhood sexual abuse.

Evidence suggests that alterations in the endogenous opiate system and dopaminergic systems are involved in the dissociative response. When the fight or flight response is not an option, as can be the case for a sexually abused child, the child freezes and surrenders. This causes the child to detach from the events, withdraw inwardly, or "go away" (Putman &

Trickett, 1997). This would be an explanation for the mental health condition known as Dissociative Identity Disorder, discussed in the previous section.

> During acute stress situations cortisol enhances survival by depressing the body's reaction to injury. ... Chronic secretions of cortisol can also depress the immune system. One of the primary organs of the immune system, the thymus gland, has been found to be significantly smaller in abused and/or neglected children when compared to those of non-abused children. The size of maltreated children's thymus glands is correlated with the severity and length of maltreatment (Fukunaga et al. 1992).

"When the trauma has ended, the feedback mechanisms are activated to counteract the stress hormones and return the heart rate, blood pressure, and other physiological adaptations to normal" (Perry, et al 1995). However, if the stress or trauma is chronic and severe, the process of the brain returning to a state of equilibrium is over activated and incapable of restoration.

Could one possibly deduce from this that, as the adult survivor of childhood sexual abuse suffering from Post Traumatic Stress Disorder experiences episodes of triggered responses, his or her brain could be experiencing a reorganization of its basal patterns of equilibrium on a regular basis through their entire life? This would be exhausting and taxing physically and emotionally. "Most researchers who study health outcomes do not consider assessing the trauma histories of research participants" (Schnurr, 2004). According to Paula P. Schnurr (2004), assessing the patient's exposure to traumatic stressors is vital to proper diagnosis. "The most common physical outcomes associated with traumatic experiences include, 1) Greater mortality, 2) Cardiovascular, cerebrovascular, and pulmonary disease, 3) Gastrointestinal disease, 4) Chronic pain, fibromyalgia, and musculoskeletal disorders, 5) Diabetes, 6) Psychogenic seizures, 7) Chronic fatigue syndrome, 8) Somatic symptoms, 9) Poorer Mental Health, 10) Lower health perceptions, 11) Lower health-related quality of life" (Schnurr, 2004).

In addition, the cost of healthcare, including outpatient visits, inpatient days, higher costs, and fewer preventative healthcare visits, can also be attributed to past abuse (Schnurr, 2004).

According to Dr. J. Douglas Bremner, from the Yale University School of Medicine, PTSD is something of an invisible epidemic. He believes that it is far more widespread than most people realize and that its underlying causes are often mysterious and always unpleasant. He also explains the physiological manifestations and emphasizes that PTSD is not just psychological (Bremner, 1997).

> ...victims actually experience physical changes to the hippocampus, a part of the brain involved in learning and memory, as well as in the handling of stress. The hippocampus also works closely with the medial prefrontal cortex, an area of the brain that regulates our emotional response to fear and stress. PTSD sufferers often have impairments in one or both of these brain regions (Bremner, 1997).

The damage done to the hippocampus, which processes memory, may well be the reason for the delayed or fragmented memories of abusive experiences. Using brain imaging, PTSD patients show a reduction in the right hippocampal volume (Bremner, 1997).

The immune system is the body's defense against all ailments. This could explain why women are more likely to seek medical attention for various illnesses and pain than men, as women are more likely to be sexually abused than men. In a study conducted by Dr. Vincent Felitti at the Department of Preventive Medicine, Southern California Permanente Medical Group, a marked reduction in physical, emotional, and vocational functioning was found among patients who reported having severe sexual trauma during childhood. He also found that sexually abused patients had significantly higher rates of chronic depression, morbid obesity, gastrointestinal problems, and recurrent headaches (Felitti, V.J., 1991).

Another condition found is pseudo-epileptic seizures (PES). They are very difficult to differentiate from actual epileptic seizures (ES). Both are "characterized by a sudden and time-limited disturbance in controlling motor, sensory, autonomic, cognitive, emotional, and/or behavioral functions" (Kuyk, Spinhoven, VanEmdeBoas, VanDyck, 1999).

Of all the medical manifestations of childhood sexual abuse, the most common illness that surfaced was chronic pain. Over the past fifteen years, researchers have learned much about the health effects of victimization. "In one recent German study, "almost all" of the community sample of female sexual abuse survivors reported pain symptoms and other somatic concerns. In fact, pain was the most commonly occurring symptom (Teegen, 1999).

Pain is a symptom that links mind and body. Finding solutions can be extremely difficult. Medications can help for a relatively short time, but can they become a permanent solution? Perhaps it would be helpful for a chronic pain sufferer to find a physician who may be experiencing the same problems. Although self-disclosure is discouraged and according to some, unprofessional, perhaps it is time for all to be **real.** Perhaps it is time for the walls to come down concerning the aftermath of childhood sexual abuse.

The most common physical problems of adult sexual abuse survivors are:

### A. Generalized Pain:

It is thought that survivors of traumatic events appear to have a lower threshold for pain due to the instability of equilibrium of the brain and the hypersensitivity to stimuli, as described above. With this lower tolerance for pain, something as simple as a hug could cause pain because the brain tells an individual that pain is occurring. This in no way means that the pain is "in one's head." The pain is most definitely real.

A survey of nearly 2,000 women showed that those who had been physically or sexually abused as children were significantly more likely than non-abused women to report physical symptoms such as back pain, stomach pain, headaches, genital pain, shortness of breath, diarrhea, and vomiting during the previous six months (McCauley et al. 1997).

### B. Headache, Back Pain, & Pelvic Pain

There is more than enough research showing that these problems are far more common among survivors than they are among the general public. "Childhood abuse has been related to the success rate of surgery for back pain" (Schofferman, Anderson, Hinds, Smith, & White, 1992). Survivors of childhood sexual abuse do not seem to heal from or receive relief after surgery.

In five independent samples of randomly selected households evaluated, the relationship between sexual assault and headaches, a symptom commonly reported by individuals with unexplained chronic fatigue, found a particularly strong association between headache and sexual assault occurring in childhood (Golding, 1999).

## C. Fibromyalgia Syndrome

Fibromyalgia Syndrome (FMS) is chronic pain that is characterized by diffuse soft tissue pain (Boisset-Pioro, Esdaile, & Fitzcharles, 1995). The research in this particular area is fairly new, as fibromyalgia is now becoming recognized as a disorder. There are clear criteria guidelines for diagnosing fibromyalgia.

A. Widespread pain in all four quadrants of the body for a minimum of three months.

B. At least 11 of the 18 specified tender points: These 18 sites used for diagnosis cluster around the neck, shoulder, chest, hip, knee and elbow regions.

Common symptoms include; fatigue, irritable bowel, sleep disorder, chronic headaches, jaw pain, cognitive or memory impairment, post-exertional malaise and muscle pain, morning stiffness, menstrual cramping, numbness and tingling sensations, dizziness or lightheadedness, skin and chemical sensitivities (Fibromyalgia Network, 2004).

One particular study completed in 1995, by Taylor, Trotter, & Csuka suggests that although the sexually abused may not have a significantly higher rate of incidence of FMS, they do report significantly more symptoms and a worse experience of pain than those who were not sexually abused (although when questioning local physicians, a definite connection is reported) (Taylor, Trotter, & Csuka, 1995). Another study also completed in the mid-1990s, found that the incidences of FMS symptoms were considerably higher in those who reported both physical and sexual abuse (Boisset-Pioro, et al., 1995). "Exposure to trauma events has also been consistently linked to chronic pain and a decreased ability to manage chronic pain. Much of this work has focused on chronic pelvic pain and fibromyalgia, both of which are associated with traumatic stressors" (Schnurr, 2004).

The researchers hypothesize that changes in the hippocampus, which deals with short-term, and long-term memory may be due to the flooding of that part of the brain with cortisol which is released during stressful events. ...It just might be possible that childhood sexual abuse as a stressor make some vulnerable people more susceptible to brain changes in the pain perception parts of the brain. Evidence is beginning to accumulate in FMS research that there are changes in these patients also. Thus it is possible that childhood sexual abuse could be one of the factors that causes FMS through its effects on the hypothalamus-pituitary-adrenal axis which controls the output of cortisol and other hormones (Burckhardt, 2004).

### D. Irritable Bowel and other Gastrointestinal Problems

The most studied pain syndrome associated with childhood sexual abuse is Irritable Bowel Syndrome (IBS). The studies completed in the early 1990's reported patients with IBS were more likely to report past sexual abuse (Drossman, et al.. 1990). Another gastrointestinal problem associated with childhood sexual abuse is Gastro Esophageal Reflux Disorder (GERD). An exorbitant amount of stomach acid, created by high stress levels, erode the walls of the esophagus. The most extreme cases can be fatal. Complicated surgeries such as "The Nissen" use part of the stomach to wrap around the base of the esophagus and stitch it in place to create a new LES to prevent acid from flowing up the esophagus. These types of surgeries are risky, but they can be lifesaving.

With the information currently available, it would be difficult for any physician to discount the effect past abuse has on the physical health of an individual.

## SPIRITUAL:

Often times, for the adult survivor of childhood sexual abuse, spirituality and sexuality link together. In families where the concept of God is present, a child's first conceptualization of God resides in the very family that has perpetrated, covered up, or just ignored the violence by which the child learns to view him or herself. If the child sees his family as loving and kind, he will also see God as loving and kind. If the family is abusive, the child's concept of God is a God that is explosive, controlling, and violent. Since a vast majority of Americans profess a belief in God or some form of a higher power, perhaps it would behoove therapists to have a working knowledge of spiritual subjects. Without discussing spirituality, none of the theories, techniques, or styles in the world will work if the patient's problems are spiritually based. For example, there are instances where the upbringing of an individual, from a spiritual or religious aspect, can have the greatest effect on how one judges or forgives herself or others. The judgment that one may impose upon herself could determine how she sees herself as good or bad, moral or immoral, just or unjust. If the father is the perpetrator and the child is raised to believe in God and believe that he is a child of God, then the concept of "God, the Father" will not be a comfort to him. He may even run from God because his image of father is abusive and degrading.

> The sexual violation of a child can have many Spiritual effects. A distorted image of God coupled with a distorted image of self creates several barriers to experiencing God's love and grace. When children are betrayed by those who were supposed to protect and love them, they find it very difficult to grasp that God loves them. Such hideous disruption of the family, making home a dangerous place, interferes with his or her sense of safety and belonging in a community of believers. God is often perceived to be punitive, an impossible taskmaster, capricious, impotent, indifferent or dead (Mandt, Langberg, 1997).

In the earlier case study of Eve, Eve was raised in the church and her extended family was in that same church. Most of Eve's early attachments were in the church. Eve's father was a leader in the church. Imagine the confusion she must have felt as her father lead songs from the pulpit and paraded the whole family to other churches to sing. Later she would lie in bed knowing that her father would have other requests of her, requests that he would not talk about at church, and requests that Eve would not talk about to anyone, as she was trained to keep secrets. Eve was trained to believe that all little girls had to do these "things" – "sexual things" – for their fathers. Eve's teachings from church were about God's love. She had to have felt that if this was God's love, she did not want any part of it. In Gordon MacDonald's book entitled *Rebuilding Your Broken World*, he describes the number of people who attend church every week with forced smiles, their secrets hidden behind those smiles. They participate in praise and worship and listen to their pastors even though the unspoken pain inside them is festering, leaving them broken and hardened. The fear of their secrets being exposed, as well as with the fear of living with their secret, freezes their emotions. This condition could last a lifetime (MacDonald, 1988).

Possibly, Eve felt that God loved everyone but her. Her teachers would tell her of the safe refuge in God, but to her, what was a safe refuge?

Eve's confusion about God and the church followed her into young adulthood. If not for the kindness and patience of her youth leader, she would have not been able to reestablish her faith as an adult.

Another patient interviewed (one who is ready to open up publicly), one patient suffering from Dissociative Identity Disorder or Multiple Personalities, was raised a devout Catholic. He was taught by his mother that he was to work constantly to please God and that if he did not, his soul would go to hell when he died. He has had many therapists in the past. They were not comfortable talking about spirituality. Therefore, they may have lacked the key skills to help him. This patient was severely sexually abused by a member of the family, as well as by someone in his neighborhood. He felt guilty for what had happened to him and these events would damn his soul to hell. In addition, since he had many identities, how many souls did he have and which one was God watching? At least two of his alter egos claimed not to believe in God and they had behaviors that, he thought, would definitely send him to hell. He first must deal with the guilt. It may take a very long time just to get him to see that the abuse was not his fault. He says, "but I let it happen." Most children are so confused about what is happening to them that they freeze. This patient has also felt guilty for early childhood sexual thoughts.

> Many survivors carry a deep sense of shame and are full of both self-blame and self-loathing. On a very deep level, many survivors think that the abuse occurred because of some innate badness within them as persons. Survivors also see themselves as powerless to make good things happen or bad things stop; at the same time, they see themselves as having excessive power to cause bad or evil in the lives of others. They will also use words like worthless, trash, or garbage when referring to themselves (Mandt Langberg, 1997).

The patient now understands that the sexual abuse perpetrated upon him awakened his sexuality before it was time. Sexuality usually does not begin blooming until adolescence. When a child is forced to learn sexual stimulation before the age of natural maturity, it can be as though he begins adolescence early. The next part of the patient's dealing with the guilt was his understanding that he did nothing to bring it on. As an exercise, he was asked to watch a five-year-old boy play and see if there was anything seductive about him. His response was that there was nothing seductive about a five-year-old boy. If there was nothing sexual about that five-year-old boy, then there was nothing sexual about him at five years old. How could the abuse be his fault if that were true? The analogy made sense to him and has helped him in his healing. His next step was to understand that he had only one soul and by his confession of faith, he was saved. When this part finally sunk in, he felt as though a burden had been lifted from him.

As can be seen from this example, childhood sexual abuse has had a profound impact on how this patient thought of himself spiritually. It was imperative, given his belief system, to reconcile his spiritual confusion. This reconciliation aided his recovery.

The mental and spiritual development of the child has a direct impact on the developing self.

> Chronic abuse in the life of the developing child has consequences that are even more profound because the experience of abuse is woven throughout the development of the self. The traumatized child grows up in a family in which caretaking relationships are severely disrupted. The primary relationships that are meant to teach us about ourselves and others in nurturing ways end up forcing the child to erect defense barriers that profoundly alter the developing self. Trauma shapes every facet of the self. The child will feel the impact of trauma physiologically, affectively, cognitively, and spiritually (Mandt Langberg, 1997).

Morals are another issue that the adult survivors of sexual abuse must face. Childhood is the time to set boundaries for life. Lives are off balance and confusing. For example, during the day a sexually abused thirteen year old girl may listen to lectures from her mother about not having sex or even letting a boy touch her in certain ways, while at night her father does those very things and tells her this is what girls are suppose to do for their fathers. Thus, these girls are confused as to the nature of "right and wrong" in matters of sexuality and intimacy.

Most people have a basic moral code within themselves. They may not be living that code, but still, they may feel some guilt because they are not living the way they know they should. The larger the gap between the way they know they should live and the way they do live can determine their peace of mind and their sense of self-worth. If that gap is created and enlarged by their family of origin, their basic moral code may cease to exist. This brings on chaos and the lack of self-discipline, which leads to poor choices. Sexually abused adolescent girls are at a higher risk of contracting sexually transmitted diseases, becoming pregnant, having multiple sex partners, alcohol and drug abuse, and sexual revictimization (Gorcey, M., Santiago, J., McCall-Perez, F. 1986). Other poor choices include relationship choices, career choices and lifestyles.

## SOCIAL/FAMILIAL:

As can be seen in Eve's case study, the disconnection from her abusive parents has enabled her recovery. Now, some may think that Eve could keep her mother in her life. If Eve's memories tell her that her mother had knowledge or encouraged the abuse, how can she see her mother in any different light than she sees her father? They are one and the same to her. The case also could be made that Eve's mother's career of babysitting children could be her providing victims for her pedophile husband. If sexual abuse occurs in a home, someone's eyes are closed. Moreover, "the most important factor in poor long term adjustment of victims was mother's anger at the child for having revealed the sexual relationship" (Bagley, Mallick, 1999).

Not all victims need total disconnection. Some feel a great need to forgive and forget. But can incest or any other form of molestation ever really be forgotten? Can one forgive, but choose to live a life free from their parents? For some victims, this inability to disconnect is the very reason they stay victims and do not move on to the survival stage. Why is disconnecting so hard for victims to do? They still want their parents to be what society portrays parents to be: positive, helpful, encouraging, and loving caregivers – in effect, an idealization. However, many grow up with what Susan Forward in her book *Toxic Parents* explains as a damaged sense of self worth. Toxic parents are parents whose negative patterns of behavior are consistent and dominant in a child's life, and they do harm. This includes the inadequate parent, the controllers, the alcoholics, the verbal abusers, the physical abusers and the sexual abusers (Forward, 1989). Though, for the purpose of this project the discussion will center around sexually abusive parents. Not all are alcoholics, but the remainder of the list applies. "Like a chemical toxin, the emotional damage inflicted by these parents spreads throughout a child's being, and as the child grows, so does the pain." What better word than "toxic" to describe parents who inflict trauma, abuse, and denigration on their children and in most cases continue to do so even after their children are grown? "There are exceptions to the "ongoing" or "repetitive" aspects of this definition. Sexual or physical abuse can be so traumatic that often a single occurrence is enough to cause tremendous emotional damage" (Forward, 1989). Continuing to bare the burdens of guilt, shame and inadequacy as adults, the development of a positive self-image is extremely difficult. "Even as adults we continue to blame ourselves for our parent's inability or unwillingness to parent protectively instead of aggressively and dominant" (Forward. 1989). The victim's desperate need, as adults, to reverse the balance of power leads to numerous lifelong problems. This may well be an excellent way to describe codependency. Codependent adults believe it is their responsibility to care for anyone that comes within their realm. If the level of caring does not happen to the codependent's satisfaction, then the codependent feels a failure. To accomplish such a task, a tremendous amount of power must be involved. This would explain the need to reverse the balance of power.

This struggle for a power position of some form in the family creates a "plastic family" – one that is very different than it appears. Based on the previously discussed statistics, nearly one-fourth of all families live a lie, and this is just the families buried in the secrets of sexual abuse. The ramifications to families are that they live lies just to look normal. They learn to create new families that will probably live lies and so the cycle is perpetuated. Lies upon lies upon lies – the "ripples" continue.

Self-esteem reflects the ability an individual has to accept or be comfortable with self and place in society. Through the sense of self, the development of contentment with personalities, bodies, attractiveness, competence, acceptance, ability to achieve, ability to receive and give love, and a basic sense of self-worth begins. According to Taylor (1991) in *The Inner Child Workbook*, these feelings are the very root of existence and are extremely important to personal development, as well as relational development.

> How you feel about yourself and your body, and how you deal with and respect the positive and negative qualities in yourself and others, are related to how you experienced these issues when you were between the ages of three and six. This period was when you began to learn the difference between good and bad behavior. When you were good (acting like the adults

in your life expected and wanted you to act), you were rewarded. When you were bad (acting in ways that were unacceptable to these adults), you were punished (Taylor, 1991).

Robson (1988) wrote that self-esteem is the sense of acceptance and contentment that allows a person's strong sense of self worth, significance, attractiveness, competence and ability to satisfy goals and aspirations. As the child grows and develops with these (sometimes) faulty perceptions, so does the sexual self.

Sexuality is not simply limited to the genitals, discrete behaviors, or biological aspects of reproduction, but also is understood as one component of the total personality that affects one's concept of personal identity and self-esteem (Whitlock & Gillman, 1989).

Children are naturally interested in exploring their own sexuality, but, if parents become involved in sex play with them, then what was once natural becomes unnatural and unhealthy.

> Our identity is shaped largely by the reflections our parents communicate to us. If these mirrors reflect love and strength, we will probably develop a healthy sense of who we are. To the degree that the mirrors reflect that we are unlovable or that our value is based on our ability to please them, then our identity will be distorted (McGee & Springle, 1992).

If pleasing the adults in one's life has anything to do with sex, the child learns to think of herself as a sexual object. If the adult involved is a family member or a perceived family member and the pleasing involves sexual gratification on the part of the adult, this is incest. If this occurs:

... the child grows up feeling disconnected from their body and may develop a pattern of sexualizing needs because, as a child the needs were responded to in a sexual manner. In adulthood, love can get confused with sex; "being run deep" (Taylor, 1991).

If the sexual self is the focus, then love can become confused with "putting out."

The wounds from incest dramatically affect the development of the child, and this child could become a sexual addict. This addiction can manifest in numerous ways that are unhealthy and sometimes very dangerous. An addiction to sex can lead one to choose professions in pornography, prostitution, or any other arena where sexual degradation may be involved.

Eby (2004) suggests that a survivor may incorporate into his self-image negative connotations such as feeling he is bad and full of shame, guilt, or being different and inferior, which could lead to behaviors associated with delinquency such as acting out, self-mutilation and substance abuse.

The act of abuse of any kind from a perceived caregiver robs that child of the opportunity to develop healthy, trusting relationships with adults. It is a major contributor to low self-esteem and impairs healthy psycho-social development. The effects of this abuse can last a lifetime (Parson, 2001). Much like physical scars from deep wounds, the emotional scars of trauma inflicted by others do not go away. These injuries may go unseen, but their scars are very real. Though the scars may not be visible on the outside, on the inside, they are devastating. According to Phillips and Daniluk (2004), the words these women use to describe themselves are "different," "alone," and "invisible." Many survivors find it very difficult to talk to anyone else about their abuse, some feeling as though they are the only one that could have experienced what they have experienced.

> Because the abuse so much defined who they were and how they felt about themselves, they believed that they had to keep themselves from being 'known.' Somewhat like imposters, the women described having experienced a sense of incongruence between how they were feeling on the inside and what others perceived from their outward appearance (Phillips & Daniluk, 2004).

Adult survivors of sexual abuse identify themselves within the context of that abuse. It is as though they are seeing themselves and the world around them through the eyes of the abused child. They not only develop feelings of self-loathing but an exorbitant amount of shame as well.

Wilson (2001) describes the concept of "blinding shame." This shame is the soul-deep belief that something is horrifically wrong that is not wrong with anyone else in the entire world. This isolation of self can cause an individual to feel as though they must do twice as much work to feel half as good. They feel literally bound by their shame, difference, and worthlessness. These feelings of shame are developed very early in life. However, they are manifested differently, dependent upon the chronological and sociological age of the individual. Feeling inferior to others, worse than any one else, significantly inhibits development of self-esteem. Shame is based upon the principle that everyone can and should be perfect. This shame not only binds us, it also blinds us.

With all that in mind, plus recalling how vital is the development of the psycho-social self, consider the sexually abused child. Consider words like: shame, doubt, self-loathing, guilt, fear of intimacy, unresolved anger, anxiety, depression, damaged goods, fear of attachments, dissociative tendencies, impaired social skills, dysfunctional relationships, abuse of substances, the need to forget, secrets, secrets, and more secrets. These words only begin to describe what is in the mind of a sexual abuse survivor. At a time before victims are old enough to accurately interpret the world around them, perpetrators are teaching these words and implanting them into the minds of their victims. Some survivors feel the need to purge the evil from self, and they can be extremely creative in their attempts.

One very important determining factor of a sexually abused young girl's self-esteem is the initial reaction she gets from her mother when the secret is revealed. Unfortunately, far too many girls get the message that

- Women do not believe what you say.
- Women do not have the power to protect their daughters.
- Women do not think sexual violation is worth "worrying about."
- A woman's job is to clean up the mess men make of our lives (Harris, 2000).

Sexual abuse within the child's family (incest) is a result of profound parental neglect. At least, one or possibly both of the parents are in denial as to the violation of their child's mind and body. This is possibly due to the parents' emotional detachment from their child. "For sexual abuse to occur within a family, there needs to be not only the abusing parent, but also a neglectful, rejecting, non-sexually abusing parent. We can wonder how incest could possibly extend over time if parents were awake, attached, and attuned to their child's behaviors and emotional life" (Pokrass, 2004). With this type of environment, how would one even hope to develop a healthy self-image. This is exactly how our case study patient, Eve, describes the feelings surrounding her family of origin. This would also explain why Eve feels the same about her mother as she does her father. One was abusive and one was blind.

As children, the perception of self is developed and that very perception can dictate the outcome of their lives in relation to that perception. As an example, let us say that a little girl understands, very early in life, that her role is her father's object of pleasure. And, without knowledge of the fact that this could be abnormal, her life is then defined as an object of pleasure or she is defined by her sexuality. Alfred Adler best describes this in his book *Social Interest.*

> Each individual is unique, and in the first seven years of life acquires a lifestyle, a kind of master plan, if you like, by which they live their life. The master plan helps give a unity to the personality and individuals see life in a unique way from their own viewpoints. The lifestyle not only includes the individual's conviction and beliefs, it organizes a person's acting, thinking and perceiving. Because the lifestyle is only in formation in the first five to seven years, the individual's subjective experience is limited and is therefore likely to be subject to either mistaken beliefs or guided by faulty perceptions, such as 'Life is cruel,' 'All people are unkind,' etc.
>
> These mistaken beliefs can be seen as a function of the individual's private logic (Adler, 1956).

Another important factor in the development of a healthy sense of self-worth is insight – insight into one's inner being. True insight involves understanding the personal truths by which one lives her life. Growing up in a home riddled with secrets does not encourage this development.

> The truth by which we live in our public worlds must be the truth by which we live in our private worlds. The gap or the difference between the two will largely determine the state of our personal health (MacDonald, 1988).

Insight, as discussed above, is dependent upon the ability to successfully integrate these two worlds. Keeping secrets, like those of the sexually abused, only stretches these two worlds farther apart. Regaining one's self-worth after surviving childhood sexual abuse must involve the resolution, or the bringing together, of these two worlds. For some this is a long and painful task, however, a task that must be taken for the development of healthy self-esteem.

Marriage, broadly defined, is the public display and the legal commitment that two individuals make toward each other, supposedly, until "death do they part." By design, marriage is the relationship in which an individual should feel total trust and loyalty. If these qualities are taught early in a child's life, this child will most likely be able to give and receive them as adults. However, for the sexually abused, especially those abused in the home of their families of origin, over long periods of time, this concept of total trust and loyalty can be impossible, or at best illusive.

> Child sexual abuse involves a breach of trust or an exploitation of vulnerability, and frequently both. Sexually abused children not only face an assault on their developing sense of sexual identity, but a blow to their construction of the world as a safe enough environment and their developing sense of others as trustworthy. In those abused with someone with whom they had a close relationship, the impact is likely to be all the more profound. A history of child sexual abuse

is reported to be associated in adult life with insecure and disorganized attachments (Alexander, 1993).

Trust and loyalty are very difficult to understand for individuals who have not grown up in loving, trusting homes. Survivors usually express their desire for this type of relationship, yet seem to be drawn to the type of partners who are incapable of meeting these needs. And, if this type of relationship is found, not knowing how to respond to and/or not feeling worthy of this type of love, survivors of sexual abuse tend to "run off the good ones." After years of being treated in a degrading fashion, believing one is worthy of the benefits of a positive relationship is extremely foreign and difficult. Human beings will more generally choose what is familiar (good, bad, or ugly), without regard to what may be in their best interest or the best interest of their potential partner. "Increased rates of relationship breakdown have also been reported in those exposed to child sexual abuse" (Beitchman et al. 1991). Most marriages fail because the couple either fails to meet the needs of one another or they make each other miserable. So it is that couples either fail to do, or they do the wrong thing. If an individual feels as though his partner is working to meet his needs, he is more likely to feel satisfied with his marriage. In Willard F. Harley, Jr.'s book entitled *His Needs Her Needs*, his explanation for most marriage failures is ignorance; ignorance as to how to recognize and meet the needs of one's spouse. He explains how men and women have difficulty understanding and appreciating the value of each other's needs. "Men tend to try to meet the needs that they would value and women do the same. The problem is that the needs of men and women are often very different and we waste effort trying to meet the wrong needs" (Harley, Jr., 1986).

Debra Susan Penrod, Ph.D.

This process can be especially difficult for the couple where one or both partners have sexual abuse in their past. It is difficult enough to understand one's own personal marital needs if one has grown up in a loving, caring home. Imagine the confusion felt by the survivors of sexual abuse. Understanding one's needs without the benefit of growing up with healthy boundaries, an ingrained sense of positive self worth, and a good working knowledge as to the appropriate roles within a family can preclude one from the possibility of understanding needs, either one's own, or someone else's. Mr. Harley also describes the love bank and how a couple makes emotional deposits and takes emotional withdrawals. They should also be cognizant as to their balances, so as not to take out more than they have deposited (Harley, Jr., 1986).

This makes perfect sense for the couple that starts out with each having a $0.00 balance. However, when one member of the relationship begins with an overdrawn balance that the other member is unaware of, problems can begin very early. The member of the relationship that has not been the recipient of past sexual abuse may feel as though they must continually make more deposits, just to keep a healthy balance. They may become resentful over time and eventually give up. This makes disclosure and intervention (described below) extremely important, as is continual communication. Real healing from sexual abuse is a lifelong endeavor.

Any kind of relationship, if successful, requires ongoing work. This task continues throughout a lifetime. In the beginning, both members in the relationship idealize each other and relate accordingly. This idealization should dissipate naturally into a healthy realization of the differences between them and how to productively work through their issues without negative consequences (Gladding, 1995). Survivors of sexual abuse often over-idealize relationships and do not expect this continual process. They see relationships as either abusive or

76

wonderful. "Most survivors do not know how to love, trust, speak the truth, and handle conflict through the normal ups and downs of human relationships" (Mandt Langberg, 1997).

The complicated dynamics upon which relationships are structured are in and of themselves a conundrum for the sexually abused. Their first relationships in life were likely to be those of their abusers or the ones who protected their abusers. The very concept of "relationship" will be foreign to them, or confusing, at best. This would include any kind of a relationship. Adding the intricacies and intimate nature of a committed partnership for life may prove illusive. In Dusty Miller's book *Women Who Hurt Themselves*, the concept of women being at war with themselves is expounded upon.

> Imagine a long, black marble wall, inscribed with names, reaching far into the distance. Imagine a quilt, covered with names and images of loved ones who have died, stretching over acres of land. But instead of war casualties and AIDS victims, the names on this wall and this quilt are those of women who died by their own hand. They died from alcoholism, drug addiction, anorexia, bulimia, excessive dieting, self-inflicted burns and slashing, and a hundred other ways of harming one's own body. These are women who killed themselves, yet they could be considered murder victims. In childhood they suffered sexual abuse, physical abuse, or psychological terrorism. Their names would stretch for hundreds of miles if inscribed on a memorial wall or stitched on a memorial quilt. These women are not remembered as brave victims of a war or an epidemic illness, but they should be. Instead, they are often blamed for their deaths because the fatal wounds were inflicted by their own hand. These wounds, however, were a direct consequence of earlier injuries

inflicted by parents, grandparents, and other primary caretakers, injuries that never healed and proved
deadly (Miller, 1994).

These women could see no way out of their despair and
pain, they had no language to describe what was happening
to them, they lived most of their lives deep within themselves
in a world of secrecy and fear, at times coping by partial
awareness. While psychologically bleeding from these wounds,
they reenact the pain inflicted upon them. This reenacting,
and reinforcing of their belief that they were incapable of
protecting themselves because they were unprotected as children, Miller refers to as "Trauma Reenactment Syndrome"
or TRS (Miller, 1994).

TRS women, whose rage, pain, and shame led them
to hurt themselves, reenact the trauma inflicted upon
them in childhood through a pattern of behaviors,
a set of distinct personality styles, and a number of
predictable and distressing problems in life (Miller,
1994).

These predictable and distressing problems are direct
contributors to the problems suffered in relationships. To
overcome these problems, the spouse of the sexually abused
must become as educated as possible about the warning signs
of TRS as well as Post Traumatic Stress Disorder (PTSD),
discussed in the Mental Health section of this project.

When the sexually abused become adults, they are more
likely to seek out relationships that mirror the relationships
of those who raised them, unless an intervention occurs. An
intervention can be therapy, spirituality, self-study, or just
sheer determination not to continue the patterns. As fathers
or mothers, we teach our children how to react to stress and

anger, how to treat a spouse, how to expect to be treated by a spouse, how to treat children, and basically, how to look at the world in general. The responsibility is immense and many are not up to the task. As children, we are subject to our own perceptions, which may or may not be true, but they are our reality. A child may be told that they are fat and stupid. This may not be real, but it becomes the child's reality.

> None of us lives by reality; we live by our perception of reality. Perceptions are never formed in a vacuum. Events and relationships combine to influence how we view circumstances. The closer and more long term a relationship we have with someone, the more effect that person's attitudes and actions will have on our world view (Springle, 1994).

Before becoming adults, the greatest influences are usually our parents or care-givers. If parents or caregivers have developed in a dysfunctional family and have taken steps of intervention not to continue negative behaviors, they should tell those they love about their pasts – admittedly a task not easily carried out. Some, due to repressed memories or fear of rejection are not able to disclose this information, information that will have a great effect on their own personal relationships. However, if the information is available it is best to reveal it. If one does not take the time to help their loved one and their self by learning to understand the past and how it effects the present, then the relationship will be less likely to succeed.

> Self-disclosure may be as scary to you as skydiving without a parachute. You hold back because you anticipate rejection or disapproval. But you miss a lot. Self-disclosure makes relationships exciting and

builds intimacy. It clarifies and enlivens. Without self-disclosure, you are isolated in your private experience (McKay, Davis, Fanning, 1995).

For some, this isolation is their norm, so as they strive to replicate their family of origin, they alienate new possible relationships. As child survivors, they were isolated in their private experiences and as adults they are isolated in their private experience, therefore, isolation is their norm.

Besides isolation, survivors, especially those with blocked memories, choose anger as a way to express themselves. However, the intensity of the anger expressed is not proportionate to the specific event, though it may be proportionate to their pasts. The individual in the relationship with a survivor of sexual abuse has now become the recipient of displaced anger. Since the survivor could not express the anger felt as a child, he or she now attempts to dump that anger on whomever they feel comfortable. "Anger provides an illusion of personal power that may temporarily block feelings of confusion and helplessness that commonly result from painful personal crises" (Wilson, 2001).

The spouse in this situation, usually not knowing about the past abuse, responds in kind. Now, we have two people fighting not really knowing about what they are fighting. Obviously, this does not lead to healthy communication nor a healthy relationship. With proper self-disclosure, the couple can identify what is really a problem between them and what is a trigger to old feelings left unexpressed.

Sexual problems in the marriage are prevalent with couples where childhood sexual abuse is involved with one of the partners. If both members were sexual abused the problems are even more compounded. A healthy sexual relationship or just a relationship of any kind requires trust. The adult survivor of sexual abuse has experienced the ultimate breach of trust and exploitation. This creates tremendous vulnerability. And being able to be vulnerable is the key to intimacy. Without the feeling of being able to be comfortable with who we are and how to express our needs to our partner, intimacy could be allusive and for some couples, impossible. The sexually abused are seldom comfortable with themselves, let alone with someone else. If the sexual abuse came from someone whom they should have been able to trust, usually a parent or parental figure, close relationships are even more difficult. This only takes into account the emotional aspects of the sexual abuse. The physical repercussions are an entirely separate issue. The greatest determinant of the physical aspects of sexual abuse is the degree and duration of the abuse.

How do we learn to become parents? Do our children come equipped with a handbook, so we are sure to do exactly what each and every particular child needs? Not only do we not have a handbook, but the handbook for each particular child would be different and the rules of life may change at any time. What is absolute in one time, may not be in another. The number one way we learn parenting skills is by remembering what our parents did when we were young. "Parents function as mirrors to their children, mirrors with messages" (Wilson, 2001). For some, this is a great place to gain the skills needed to be good parents to help children become productive adults. If this were the case, they would be modeling the positive skills of parenting. If the model of a parent is abusive, there is a greater chance of becoming like them. One may say that they will never be anything like their parents. However, without making a conscious choice to be different, the behavior will be modeled and the abused becomes the abuser.

Another aspect of parenting for survivors is the mental stability of the survivor. Not only have they learned poor parenting skills, but they also bring their "old baggage," unresolved emotional problems, to the situation. Depending upon how well their past abuse has been remembered and treated, parental decisions could be hampered. For example, if the adult survivor of childhood sexual abuse is still in a denial stage, he may not be able to put the needs of his child first; indeed his own needs could be paramount. This would produce a very selfish parent and a child who feels ignored. This would then lead to a child feeling as though she was not valued, which would result in low self-esteem and a feeling *that she could never do enough for anyone.* In this example, although the survivor did not abuse his child in the same way that he was abused, some of the same outcomes would occur.

Another example would be the parent who does remember her own abuse, but has not sought treatment. This example would be a very angry parent, one who could project that anger onto her spouse or children. Either way the outcome would be negative for the child. Children who grow up with absentee or angry parents lack the first basic need of a child, which is security.

Even survivors who have accepted their past and sought treatment may lack all the skills for child rearing. It is imperative for these parents to have a healthy support system around them. The key is to be aware, consciously, how our past effects today and our futures.

Prescott (2002) suggests that 65 to 70 percent of women who have been abused are permanently damaged. Perhaps this is why so many children disconnect from their families of origin, and those permanently damaged mothers go on to, in some ways, damage their own children. The sad part is that they probably do not even know how or why they treat their children the way they do.

"In hurting and hurtful families, children learn that it is not safe to put their identities on the line. Their real needs and feelings are bothersome and bad. It isn't safe to show them because parents are absorbed in their own needs and feelings" (Wilson, 2001). Self-absorption is contradictory to good parenting. If a parent does have past issues of abuse that are unresolved emotionally through some form of intervention, they may be lacking in some vital areas of parenting. Even the best of parents can at times be unwilling or unavailable. If the skills of willingness, availability and unconditional love go untaught, this conscious choice involves a great deal of work and commitment.

> Many times, survivors who are parenting are fearful of abusing their own children. I have listened to several men and women who were terrified that they had abused their children when they were small and simply had no memory of it. Such thoughts are torturous (Mandt Langberg, 1997).

One of the overriding behaviors of a fearful parent is to do nothing. For the child of the "do nothing parent," the message is sent that they are not worth having anything done for them, so they must be worth nothing. Sometimes, this fear leads to the inability to stop the cycle of abuse, therefore another generation has their safety, security, and stability stolen. When the sexual safety is stolen, sexual innocence is lost once again.

The recovering survivor needs to be aware of how his recovery inhibits his parenting time. He must not allow his own pain to distract him or to allow the pain to demand all the emotional energy needed to parent. A parent distracted by the pain of his own unseen hurts notices neither his children's successes nor their problems. This is definitely the unavailable parent (Wilson, 2001).

The issue of control will continue through all stages of parenting. The survivors need for control could be stifling for their children. All children need space, with boundaries, to develop. They need the freedom to experience pain, love, rejection, pleasure, and many more feelings and experiences. A controlling parent may want to shelter her child from negative experiences or she may want to make all the decisions for the child, without her child's input. As a child ages, more and more choices will be presented. If a child's perception is that all of these choices are made by a controlling parent, their future family relationships could be damaged.

# CHAPTER 6

## HISTORY OF CHILD
## SEX ABUSE LAWS,
## THE LEGAL PROCESS, AND
## SENTENCING PROCEDURES

I n order to fully understand the history of child sex abuse
laws, we first must understand the climate of current
thought within which they were developed. Greater detail
will follow, but basically child abuse laws were developed in
the early 1900's and child sex abuse laws were introduced in
the 1960's. During this time period, 1900-1970, our adult
population would have been influenced in the area of child's
rights by early psychological theorists along with other scientists who wrote about child abuse and more specifically,
child sexual abuse.

Sigmund Freud, one of the founding fathers of psychological thought, believed initially that childhood sexual abuse
was a major precedent for the development of the emotional
problems suffered by adults. However, as his experiences with
patients grew, he had problems believing that sexual abuse
occurred so often. Therefore, he decided that children were
born with sexual wishes and desires, and thus, what they

thought "memories" were, in fact, fantasies. Sexual abuse, Freud thought, did not happen very much. (Francher, 1973). From 1938 to 1947, Dr. Alfred Kinsey, founder of the Kinsey Institute was critically acclaimed for his research in human sexuality. He was also controversial, in that these studies involved experiments on and observations of children. Both researchers drew some of the same conclusions. They differed slightly, in that Kinsey reported that adult to child sex only caused harm if the other adults surrounding the child made them feel that the act was wrong or bad (Kinsey, 1953). The Kinsey Report, as his study became known, was utilized as a base for the sexual beliefs of the past few generations and has influenced design for sexual abuse laws.

> The Revolutionary 'Kinsey Reports,' as they came to be known, including his companion volume released in 1953, Sexual Behavior in the Human Female, rocked the nation's beliefs about itself. But perhaps most shocking of all were his 'findings' on childhood sexuality: The Kinsey Reports came to the conclusion that children are sexual from birth, and that youngsters as young as a few months of age have the capacity for a pleasurable and healthy sexual life (Kupelian, 2004).

Why was Kinsey so important in this field? He and his colleagues were the only ones who dared write about such a taboo topic. It is possible that Kinsey was revered due to his boldness, and not for his content.

Explaining Kinsey's research, Eric Ericson (2000) wrote:

> In 1938, Alfred Kinsey began interviewing 20,000 Americans about numerous aspects of their sexual behavior. Describing this monumental undertaking in *Sexual Behavior in the Human Male* (and *Sexual*

*Behavior in the Human Female*), he saw himself as a disinterested scientist whose sole purpose was to uncover the facts about 'what people do sexually, and what factors account for differences in sexual behavior among individuals, and among the various segments of the population.' Trained as an etymologist, Kinsey had spent the first half of his career collecting gall wasps. Interviewing people about their sexual histories seemed to be just another kind of collecting, and he sought the widest variety of histories just as he had sought the widest variety of wasps. 'Modern taxonomy,' Kinsey pontificated, 'is the product of an increasing awareness among biologists of the uniqueness of individuals, and the wide range of variation which may occur in any population of individuals.' Thus Kinsey interviewed numerous persons whose sexual tastes differed from the average (Ericksen, 2000).

There were those who thought that Kinsey began this project just to satisfy and justify his own variety of sexual interests. However, by presenting himself as a scientist in pursuit of knowledge, he was able to proceed. He suggested that those who opposed him were standing in the way of scientific progress. It was not until the mid 1980's that someone dared to question how some of these studies were performed (Reisman & Eichel, 1990). As can possibly be seen from the following research, "science is never just a neutral endeavor. Scientists participate in the creation of culture, and they do so from a perspective that rests on their social locations and their educations as well as their ability to see things differently than those who came before" (Ericksen, 2000). This article goes on to say that as Kinsey was influenced by his restrictive upbringing, his work had a profound impact on the very behavior he studied. "Kinsey changed the sexual culture of America forever" (Ericksen, 2000).

According to Jim Keith in his article, "Sex Experiments of Alfred Kinsey," Kinsey was influenced by some unseemly individuals such as Ernst Rudin, who was to become the head of the Nazi Racial Hygiene Society, and Aleister Crowley, "the Great Beast," known in the press as the wickedest man alive. Kinsey is also linked to occultists film maker, Kenneth Anger, American Nazi, George Sylvester Viereck, and French pedophile Rene Guyon. It is suggested that "Kinsey needed the excuse of research to validate his twenty-four-hour-a-day obsession with sex" (Keith, 2005).

In his article, "The Case Against Kinsey," David Kupelian reports that Kinsey's research showed that, while American men pretend to be faithful and monogamous, most were not, 85 percent had sex prior to marriage, nearly 70 percent had sex with prostitutes, 30-45 percent had extramarital affairs, and 10-37 percent of men had engaged in homosexual acts, all of which were illegal in the early 1900's.

It is quite possible that Kinsey's greatest critic is Dr. Judith Reisman, president of the Institute for Media Education. According to Dr. Reisman, Kinsey solicited and encouraged pedophiles in the U.S. as well as other countries to sexually violate from 317 to 2,035 infants and children in order to collect his data on child sexuality. These are very serious allegations, however there seems to be little information questioning Dr. Kinsey until Dr. Reisman began, some thirty years after Kinsey's work. Oddly enough, these crimes against children are quantitatively shown in Kinsey's own graphs and charts. Why were they not challenged, especially "Table 34"? The infamous "Table 34" from *Sexual Behavior of the Human Male*, is a chart explaining how many orgasms a particular age group can have in a specific period of time. The age ranges on this particular table are from six months to ten years of age.

Reisman begs to offer the question as to how that could be determined unless by manipulation of these children, unless by molestation of these children?

> Americans bestow authority and billions of tax dollars upon science in the belief that scientists will make important contributions to society. There is the further belief that scientists, in their responsibility and trust, will behave ethically, especially in research that involves human subjects. While the former is certainly historically accurate, such trust in the class 'scientists' as honest humane persons who deserve unquestioned public faith is sustained neither by cross-cultural or American science history (Reisman & Eichel, 1990).

Reisman also asks the question, what if all Kinsey's work was fraudulent, or worse? What if it reflects unethical scientists conducting unprosecuted criminal acts?

In an unprecedented event on July 23, 1981, Reisman delivered a paper entitled, "The Scientist as a Contributing Agent to Child Sexual Abuse: A Preliminary Study,"

> ...in which she brought up for the first time in the 32 years since it had been published, the material on child sexuality in Tables 30-34 of the Kinsey Male volume and wondered how this data could have been obtained without involvement in criminal activity. Before giving her report, Reisman had written to Male Volume co-author Paul Gebhard to ask about the data in Tables 30-34. Gebhard wrote back saying that the data had been obtained from parents, school teachers, and some male homosexuals, including 'some of Kinsey's men' who had used 'manual and oral techniques' to

catalogue the number of orgasms they said they could stimulate in infants and children (Kupelian, 2004).

It has also been suggested in numerous articles that nearly three quarters of Kinsey's data was actually trashed, thus the claim that this research was based upon "normal" males may not be quite correct. In fact, estimates state that about 86 percent of these males would not have been considered "normal," even by today's standards. Reisman suggests that, of the male population used for research to show America what they should consider "normal," this 86 percent included 200 sexual psychopaths, 1,400 sex offenders and hundreds each of prisoners, male prostitutes and promiscuous homosexuals (Kupelian, 2004). Kupelian goes on to say that although Kinsey claimed that the information on child sexuality came from multiple sources, in 1995, then Kinsey Institute director John Bancroft insisted that it all came from the serial pedophile, Rex King, who was ultimately convicted of the murder of a ten-year old girl and the sexual abuse of nearly 200 children (Kupelian, 2004).

In a biography written by pro-Kinsey author, James H. Jones, in 1997, Jones revealed that changing America's sex laws was exactly what Kinsey had intended. "He wanted to undermine traditional morality to soften the rules of restraint...Kinsey was a crypto-reformer who spent his every waking hour attempting to change the sexual mores and sex offender laws of the United States" (Jones, 1997).

In summation of David Kupelian's article:

> ...today virtually everything having to do with sex-from attitudes toward extramarital sex and homo-sexuality, to the nation's sex-education curricula, to the ways medicine, psychiatry, psychology, and even the criminal justice system define and deal with sex

crimes-is rooted firmly in the ludicrously fraudulent 'data' of Kinsey and his cult of criminal deviant sex 'researchers' (Kupelian, 2004).

Whether or not one reveres Kinsey, one must acknowledge that, given his proclivity toward unusual sexual activities, his so-called "research" was tainted. He produced a study of child/adult sexuality that was unconscionable. His deductions made with tables 30-34 of *Sexual Behavior of the Human Male* must have involved adult stimulation to infants, as well as prepubescent children. This, by any interpretation, is child molestation. With no public outcry, he continued, and these same techniques were implemented for his production of *Sexual Behavior of the Human Female*. Enough of what others have said of him. Let us hear from Alfred C. Kinsey, himself.

There are, yet, insufficient data either in our own or in other studies, for reaching general conclusions on the significance of sexual contacts between children and adults. The females in the sample who had had pre-adolescent contacts with adults had been variously interested, curious, pleased, embarrassed, frightened, terrified, or disturbed with feelings of guilt. The adult contacts are a source of pleasure to some children, and sometimes may arouse the child erotically and bring it to orgasm. The contacts had often involved considerable affection and some of the older females in the sample felt that their pre-pubescent experience had contributed favorably to their later socio-sexual development...If a child were not culturally conditioned, it is doubtful if it would be disturbed by sexual approaches of the sort which had usually been involved in these histories. It is difficult to understand why a child, except for its cultural conditioning, should be disturbed at having its genitalia touched, or disturbed at seeing the genitalia of other persons, or disturbed at even more specific sexual contacts (Kinsey, 1953).

When it comes to America's culture, law, beliefs and attitudes regarding sex, Kinsey is still revered by the majority of academics and experts.

Is it possible that Dr. Alfred C. Kinsey and his so-called research spawned an entire generation of pedophiles who produced a massive generation of victims? If this was his intention, he succeeded: as quoted earlier, one of every three females and one of every six males are molested by the age of eighteen.

In our case study, Eve falls into the age bracket of being a child of those adults and parents influenced by the work of Kinsey. Eve had no knowledge of cultural norms, or sex, or anything involved with sex. This was not discussed in her home or church. There was no one to teach her about "good touch, bad touch." It is doubtful if Eve had any cultural conditioning, other than "it was her father's job to teach her about sexual things and that little girls must keep secrets."

Now that the culture and beliefs of the time period have been explored, let us move on to the actual history of the laws.

At the end of the Middle Ages, a young girl could consent to having sex with an adult when she was ten to twelve years of age. If a sexually abused girl was brought to someone's attention, she was considered the perpetrator of adultery (Wikipedia, 2006).

In 1874 there were no laws on the books to protect children, however, there were laws to protect animals. The first child abuse case was tried using the law protecting animals. The Society of Prevention of Cruelty to Animals helped a nurse in New York remove Mary Ellen, a nine year old, who was being severely abused by adoptive parents, from her home.

This case became a great media event and groups were formed to protect children. However, it was not until 1968 when Dr. Henry Kempe and Ray Helfer published "The Battered Child" that people finally started to believe that children were abused by their parents. It took another twenty years for child sexual abuse to raise attention. In 1986, Congress passed the Child Abuse Victims' Rights Act, which gave a civil damage claim to child victims of violation of sexual exploitation law (The Awareness Center, 2004).

The following is the State of Indiana's Penal Code for sentencing procedures. This is a representation of most states. The actual sentencing of offenders may differ from state to state and from county to county.

## STATE OF INDIANA PENAL CODE CLASSIFICATIONS & MINIMUM SENTENCES:

**According to Information maintained by the Office of Code Revision Indiana Legislative Services Agency:**

Class A Felony Murder: 45 years
Class A Felony: 20 years
Class B Felony: 6 years
Class C Felony: 2 years
Class D Felony: 6 months

Class A Misdemeanor: not more than 1 year + fine
Class B Misdemeanor: not more than 180 days + fine
Class C Misdemeanor: not more than 60 days + fine

Dependent upon the degree to which the child was molested, the punishment can fall into any of the above categories. Each state places a distinct difference upon whether the child has been penetrated, where they were penetrated, what they were penetrated with, the degree of force, the manner of coercion used, the physical damage done, the duration of the abuse, the age of the child, the perpetrators relationship to that child, fondling under the clothes or above the clothes, and the like. Although, the law makes such a distinction among these physical facts, most of the child's damage is psychological and can be a delayed reaction, sometimes delayed for years. The laws reflect the physical and sexual nature of abuse. However, sexual abuse has more to do with power and domination than it has to do with sex. If, perchance, this were truly understood by the general public and the criminal justice system, would punishments change? Sadly, punishments usually are decided with plea bargains that fall somewhere in the vicinity of a Class D Felony and a Class A Misdemeanor. All over the country, women are in support groups talking about their abuse, but are they talking about the exact nature of the details of that abuse, or how they feel about the loss of power and control they now feel in their lives? Perhaps, this is a mental crime as much as it is a physical one and should be punished as such.

Therapists often find themselves in the position of reporting abuse. Perhaps, not on the first visit, but at some point during therapy, therapy that is appropriate to the child's age and cognitive abilities, the counseling setting is usually where they feel safe enough to reveal childhood sexual abuse. Sometimes they are unsure of what to call it, but they know when something has happened that is not appropriate. Drawings, paintings, dolls or just general play activities are the catalyst for disclosure.

It can be extremely frustrating for therapists and other professionals to be required to report any abuse that a child may tell them and then watch the legal system decide whether to press charges after they have interviewed the offending parent. This could put the child or the professional in danger of retaliation. The ramifications of the process can be more devastating than the molestation. The child may feel molested all over again.

> All interventions should have the goal of treating children's' best interests for therapy and family integration as primary; including punitive pursuit of alleged offenders are of secondary importance. Delay of therapy for a child until a criminal trial is over, and requiring a child to undergo cross-examination are often counter productive for the child. ...Decline in mental health and self-confidence was also linked to long delays before a court case, and unsympathetic interviewing and processing of the victim (Bagley, Mallick, 1999).

To challenge this statement, why is integration of the family primary to punitive pursuits? If this family is one of (known) sexual abuse, the sexual abuse that is yet to be revealed will be of a much greater magnitude. Why throw this mess back in the same pile? What does this say to the child about her worth? The answers to these questions should be easy to ascertain, however, our society has shown that ignorance or denial as to the degree of damage to the child is a much easier response. Perhaps, this is because adult survivors and victims stay quiet. Their silence perpetuates the myth that they have adjusted; they are living "plastic lives" in a society of ignorance. Perhaps, this is a mental crime as much as it is a physical crime and should be punished as such.

> Child abuse is uniquely difficult to prosecute. No other type of case consistently presents such complex psychological and social dynamics. No other type of case so often requires the prosecutor to go to trial with

a child as its crucial witness. The pressure on victims is also uniquely painful (APRI, 2004).

Definite problems arise when children are the main witness. Some say that children live in a fantasy world and cannot be believed. Others say that children never lie about these types of issues. The answer probably lies somewhere in the middle. Like adults, children can be confused and deceived. "However it is rare for children to deliberately lie about abuse except to minimize its frequency or deny its actual occurrence" (APRI, 2004). Specialized training for all those involved in the case will cause the least amount of trauma to the child.

The accuracy with which a child can remember and describe what has happened to him is dependent upon three processes of the memory:encoding, storage, and retrieval. The age of the child as well as the elapsed time since the victimization, to a great degree, determine how well these complex processes function for that child. Children have a higher degree of difficulty understanding complex events, relationships, feelings, and intentions. If a child has difficulty understanding an event, the memory is not encoded correctly. A child who has not been taught correct terminology for the human body will not have the vocabulary to explain exactly what has happened to them. They may refer to the penis as a snake, a stick, or the name their perpetrator gave them for that body part. If an event or a part of the body has not been encoded correctly, it will be stored incorrectly and not be available for proper retrieval later. Without training and expertise in this area of understanding children, the crime will likely go unpunished.

"The legal system was not designed for children. In fact, the investigative and legal response to child maltreatment may have a traumatic effect upon the child" (Sagatun & Edwards, 1995).

Since, there is such a distinction as to the sexual act and the punishment assessed, there must be some precedent or significant influence from which these ideas have been derived.

In most reported cases, substantiation is difficult to ascertain. The process becomes simpler either by dropping the case due to lack of evidence or by sentence modifications or plea bargaining. This lessening of the punishment serves the court system in that money is saved by not having to try the case, time is saved by the attorneys with bargaining, but mostly the victim is left to feel invalidated and invisible.

These statements assume that incest has negative effects for the victim. However, this belief is not shared by all professionals in the relevant fields. In one of his controversial works, *Sexual Behavior in the Human Female*, Alfred Kinsey argued that child-adult sexual contact was in itself not nearly so harmful as the shame induced by outraged conservative adults (Kinsey, 1938). Does this mean that a sex-act is only wrong when it is offensive to one of the parties involved? This argument assumes that a child has the ability to logically agree to sex. Another assumption is that all parents or child caretakers know what is best for the children involved. Perhaps, statistics will answer these questions.

Looking at the statistics of an issue that, itself could be "the dirty little secret," in many families is a confusing and difficult task.

> We don't see sexual abuse because of the dynamics of denial and because of the nature of these abuses. Sexual abuse doesn't announce itself. Like other forms of abuse, it is about power and control. The abuser systematically disempowers, humiliates, and isolates his/her victim. Abusers often threaten to harm the victim more if s/he tells, or to harm people the victim loves. Unlike some forms of abuse, molestation generally

happens in private, without witnesses. In addition, children are often too young to have the concepts of language to describe what has been done to them. Without those concepts or language, their attempts to tell are often misunderstood, minimized, ignored, or dismissed... and it gets easier to see why the violation of children is often unseen and why children keep silent (Lev, 2003).

Most statistics depend upon visible proof of the abuse. However, childhood sexual abuse usually leaves no visible scars. Beatings leave bruises, knifings leave wounds, but the pain endured by sexual abuse victims is internal. "They are damaged by a violation of trust more profound than any violation of the body. They are scarred by a premature loss of childhood innocence that prevents them from becoming healthy adults" (Brunni, 2002).

Statistics can also be polluted with false reporting and false memory syndrome. False reporting can occur during child custody cases when one spouse is trying to discredit the other or when children have learned to manipulate their parents and the legal system in order to meet their own agenda (Keating, 2000).

There is also the notion that people need something or someone upon which to blame their bad behaviors, and that claiming sexual abuse has become a popular "attention getter" for this purpose. On the other hand, "some believe that, for the first time in history, we are beginning to face the true prevalence and significance of child abuse. Others worry that many people have become obsessed with child abuse and deny any personal responsibility while 'blaming' them on abuse and bad parenting" (Hopper, 2004). "While child abuse has always been present, our country has only recently begun to intervene on behalf of abused children" (Sagatun,

Edwards, 1995). There is an old saying that figures lie and liars figure, so great care must be taken when analyzing statistics. Childhood sexual abuse is an even more difficult area to analyze. The reason being is that most children never tell anyone about the abuse, especially when their sexual abuser is someone within their home.

> Ninety percent of all incest victims never tell anyone what has happened, or what is happening, to them. They remain silent, not only because they are afraid of getting hurt themselves, but to a great extent because they are afraid of breaking up the family by getting a parent into trouble. Incest may be frightening, but the thought of being responsible for the destruction of the family is even worse. Family loyalty is an incredibly powerful force in most children's lives, no matter how corrupt that family may be (Forward, 1989).

Another reason this area is so difficult to analyze and treat is children often block the abuse from their minds and may not remember the specific events for many years. Having a parent abuse the trust and reliance that their child has developed with them is so traumatic that the child is at a loss as to how to process this information. The human mind is remarkable, if an event happens that is too difficult, the mind tucks that memory away to deal with it when the individual is more equipped to understand what has happened.

Several years ago, the cover story of the August 15, 1983 issue of *Time Magazine* reported on a number of studies investigating infants' memories of events. The result of their studies reported by Seamands (1985) was that babies know a great deal more than was expected. They see, hear, and understand more than had been thought before. They also found that babies are genetically prewired to make friends with any adult who cares for them. This makes them extremely vulnerable to the motives, needs, and desires of that caregiver. One of the most important findings of the study was that before an infant can speak, he is thinking, learning, and remembering. Intellect is at work before any language is available as a tool (Seamands, 1985).

No one person is alike as to how he recovers his memories, but the most common way is to begin with flashbacks brought on by a trigger of some kind. A trigger can be a setting, an event or even something as insignificant as a smell. The flashbacks usually begin gradually and may take years to unfold. Most women never fully retrieve all memories, but not everything must be brought to the conscious memory stage for an individual to have a good idea what has happened to them. They also do not need all of their memories to move from victim to survivor. Hamer (2002) wrote that a flashback is described as "a symptom, one which indicates the fact that damage to the mind has been sustained some time before" (Hamer, 2002). Trauma is described as a whole body event, so the whole body is affected.

"Under the strain of attempting to absorb an experience that it cannot assimilate or organize, the whole system becomes overwhelmed and goes down." This neurological damage, Hamer writes, can be measured. It is as though the central nervous system has been broken into fragments (Hamer, 2002).

> Incest hurts not only during the time it happens. When undiscovered, ignored, discounted, minimized, or disbelieved it hurts that person throughout her life. Sexual molestation hurts the child, the adult she becomes, and those who love her... Unresolved trauma of any kind leaves it's legacy in future generations (Lev, 2003).

# CHAPTER 7

## SUMMARY AND RECOMMENDATIONS

Although Child Protection Services is the primary agency responsible for protecting children and investigating complaints, the task is not solely up to them. According to the "Investigation and Prosecution of Child Abuse" (a training manual for Prosecutors and those involved in child abuse cases), the cooperation of many different agencies is required to adequately do the best job for the child. Agencies involved include law enforcement, child protection, medical, and mental health professionals. These agencies must coordinate efforts and share information. This cooperation of professionals can minimize the number of times the child must undergo an interview, thus minimizing additional trauma (APRI, 2004). In order to have a greater understanding of the work involved with the legal community, it seemed necessary to get opinions from representatives of such. A specific group of questions concerning sexual abuse was chosen.

The primary questions used for interviewing criminal justice personnel can be found as the appendix of this project. Interviewee's include a judge, a prosecutor, an attorney, and a representative of Child Protections Services. The following is a summary of those interviews.

The process from reporting to prosecution is as follows:

1) A report is made to Child Protection Services. That report may come from an individual, a school, a therapist, a doctor, or any other person or professional who has contact with a child.

2) A representative from Child Protection Services interviews the parents of the child in an attempt to determine if a case can be substantiated.

3) The child is interviewed by an investigator from Child Protection Services. An investigator from local law enforcement may also be present or may conduct his or her own interview.

4) The information gleaned from these interviews is used to determine if a prosecutable case can be attempted.

5) If this information is considered credible, the case is sent to the Prosecutor's office for review.

6) The Prosecutor's office repeats the interviews and makes its own determination if it thinks a case can be prosecuted.

7) If all information is deemed worthy, formal charges are filed.

8) The defendant's attorney and the Prosecutor entertain plea bargain possibilities.

9) If a plea bargain is not reached, the case is tried before the court and a ruling is made. However most cases are settled with a plea bargain.

The perspective of all the professionals interviewed for this project proved to be very different. There seemed to be little communication between these offices except as described above. For example, the judge seemed to have no idea how many cases were reported versus the number of cases brought to trial. There were also differing opinions as to the reunification of the family, recovered memories, the success of treatment for offenders, and as to the toughness of penalties to offenders. All seemed to agree that the bulk of the cases reported were fondling and the legal process does not favor children and probably does them more harm. Another similarity was concerning the investigation of the pasts of child sex offenders. All seemed to think this activity should be increased. All of these professionals were aware of the negative "ripple effect" to the families of the victim and to society as a whole. They were also very compassionate towards the victim and their families, but seemed confined as to their particular area of expertise. All of these professionals seemed frustrated and confined by our current system regarding child sexual abuse.

One specific county in Indiana was chosen to use as an example for statistics. This county has a population of approximately 122,000 people, including approximately 43,000 households. The median age is about thirty-six years old. A five-year-period was chosen, 2001-2006. The number of cases reported to Child Protection Services for some form of child sexual abuse during this timeframe was 509. From this number, only seven cases had charges filed. Of these seven cases one individual was sentenced to seventy-five years in prison and five individuals received probation. One of the probationers violated his probation being around young children and received two years in prison. What happened to the other 502 reports? Those children, who were brave enough to tell someone, must feel extremely unimportant. Where is their support or validation? The sad part is, this 509 is only a small portion of the actual cases of child sex abuse because most is never reported. The problem seems to lie between Child Protection Services and the Prosecutor's office. Reports are made and when charges are filed a ruling is made. Who decides the validity of a report? This is an area that should be made known to the public, perhaps then, changes would occur.

If this county is representative of the rest of the country, and I believe it is, what does this say about our current legal system? However, the problem may not lie with the legal community, but with the difficulties in professionals feeling as though they have enough evidence to try a case or if the child involved will be considered a credible witness. In the cases referred to above, the only one who received serious jail time was one in which penetration was proven. Perhaps, a new system that reflects the seriousness of abuse other than penetration, like fondling, should be considered. The research has shown that life-long negative effects occur with fondling victims. For a change as this to occur, adult survivors must develop a collective voice, *a loud collective voice.* This will only begin when stigmas are shattered and the silence is broken.

What does this mean for society? If crimes are punishable directly proportionate to the injury done to the individual and thus to society, is our current system even close to what it needs to be? Based on the long-term effects to survivors of childhood sexual abuse discussed earlier in the project, the financial cost to society is immeasurable – non-productivity, lost work hours, job changes, disability claims and more increase costs. The emotional loss to society is the lack of trust and trustworthiness. Perhaps, the county studied was just a fluke and not indicative of the rest of America. In fact, these statistics are a slap in the face to the sixty million Americans who are adult survivors of childhood sexual abuse. Is there hope for change? If so, it is up to these survivors. If change does not occur, the legacy left behind is unspeakable. It will not be pleasant or easy, however the alternative insures no change will occur. The silence must be broken.

I began this project with one directional hypothesis and four sub-positions.

**Directional Hypothesis:** Child sexual abuse penalties should be significantly more rigorous in order to prevent an individual who is not likely to be rehabilitated from offending again. Furthermore, our current legal system does not punish offenders relative to the serious impact perpetrated upon the victims.

**Sub Positions:**

1) Child sexual abuse permanently, dramatically and adversely impacts victims' lifelong functioning.

2) Most adult child sexual abusers are untreatable.

3) Child sex offenders are likely to re-offend despite the imposition of our current legal sentencing guidelines.

4) Child sex offenders are likely to re-offend under our current legal procedures for sentence modification.

I believe the reliability of these statements has been supported with the research. I offer the following as recommendations for change:

A) <u>More rigorous penalties:</u> The penalties in cases where actual penetration has occurred seem close to adequate, however, the gap between those and the cases of fondling is immense. This crime should warrant more than four years, which in most cases end with the majority of the time spent on probation. Given the research of this project concerning the lifelong problems of survivors of any kind of childhood sexual abuse, including fondling, perhaps sentencing for this crime should reflect the damage done. An educated public should agree with more rigorous penalties.

Instead of this crime falling under the category of a class A misdemeanor or a class D felony, this crime should at a minimum warrant a class A or B felony. This would insure a lengthy jail term where treatment could commence.

B) <u>Educate the legal community regarding the damage done to victims of all forms of childhood sexual abuse:</u> The sentencing for child sex offenders should be relative to the damage done to the victims. This would require all the legal system involved to be educated as to the life-long problems suffered by the survivors of all forms of sexual abuse. Again, this would definitely include survivors speaking out, first to the legal community then the public. Once survivors are ready to speak up, this could begin with a series of public service announcements along with a survivors' lecture series, as well as in-service training for individuals involved in all areas of the system.

C) <u>Educate the public regarding the damage done to victims of all forms of childhood sexual abuse:</u> The education of the public regarding the damage done to victims could occur through a series of lectures. These lectures could begin in churches and service organizations. The mental health community must be involved, as these lectures would inevitably bring up past memories of those in attendance and treatment providers would be needed for those individuals. This process could begin inexpensively and simply with one survivor in their area of the country with their sphere of influence. They would find and train at least one other survivor who continues the process with their circle of influence and so on.

D) <u>The treatment of child sex offenders:</u> Currently our only way of knowing the effectiveness of treatment is to place the offender into society with children and then wait to see if they will re-offend. This is leaving children to fend for themselves while we wait. If sentencing is involved, at least ten years in jail along with treatment, and the testing of offenders to determine their possible reentry into society, re-offending would be rare. The testing used would be based upon the recent work by Illes (2001), the Stanford Medicine Magazine in the fall of 2005. The trial studies were carried out by Scott Atlas, MD and professor of radiology at Stanford University (Atlas, 2005). The MRI studies the blood rushing to specific portions of the brain based on specific stimuli. The sample tests used pedophile and non-pedophile men. Both groups were shown child pornography and both groups showed blood flow activity to the portion of the brain involving sexuality, however, when the child pornography was over, the non-pedophile men returned to normal brain wave activity, but the pedophile men continued heavy brain wave activity for an extended period of time (Adams, 2005). This test would determine the success of child sex offender treatment, and if the offender could not test within the group whose brain function returned to normal, then the offender would not reenter society.

E) <u>Plea-bargains for child sex offenders:</u> Plea bargaining for child sex offenders invalidates the victim. The victim was not given a means to negotiate what was being done to her. Perhaps, there should be a minimum time served as well as the testing discussed above or perhaps, this is a crime that should not have the option of plea bargaining. In doing the research for this project, it was found that plea bargaining is the norm – seldom do cases actually go to trial. This may save money, but, at what cost to society? This practice does prevent children from testifying and being traumatized even more, however, are they traumatized later by feeling invalidated? I propose the ten-year minimum time served and testing before reentering society.

F) Break the silence: Before the organization of Mothers Against Drunk Driving (MADD), deaths due to alcohol related traffic accidents were double what they are now. That group has had a serious impact on drunk-driving laws, in fact laws have changed drastically due to the impact of MADD. This organization spawned from one individual's loss and pain. It is my position that one person can have that same impact on child sex abuse laws. The process described above with affecting one's circle of influence, training, then repeating the process over and over until all have heard is a way of reversing the "ripple effect".

This project has shown how ripples have become waves of destruction for the survivors of childhood sexual abuse. Perhaps, it is finally time to turn those waves around. Perhaps, survivors are finally ready to reverse the balance of power.

Though many survivors succumb to the lifelong, devastating effects, some survive. We survive to praise, to love, to be loved, to help, to heal, to give, and to receive. We survive to live. Even with all that we have lost, we can use the gifts and talents that God has given us and we will fight this fight. Let us not fight alone or in vain, help. There are many Eve's all around you. Perhaps, they are more evident now and you will take the time to look. Now that you have knowledge, how will you respond?

# EPILOGUE
# OTHER VOICES CRY OUT

This section of the project is an attempt to pay tribute to the innocence lost by those struggling to survive. These excerpts were written by others who have been treated for childhood sexual abuse. There is not much order here, some are titled, some are not, but that is just a reflection of their lives. The ages vary, some are very young, as can be seen by the writings. All desire to be heard.

**Darkness**

I'm swimming all alone in a pool of darkness and I feel like darkness is slowly pulling me under. I yell for help, but no one is there to hear it. I begin to see the water at eye level and I kick and flail, fighting to stay above the darkness. But, the darkness won't let go of it's hold on me and I slowly begin to give in to the feeling that lies below the water line. The water starts to fill my lungs, the lungs that once held so much life, yet now they allow the murky water to replace it. I know this path doesn't lead to happiness, but why doesn't someone grab my hand and pull me from darkness's grasp? Because no one knows I stand at the boundary, the boundary between light and dark. So, I give in to that thing that holds me. All of the strength and all of the courage that I once held in my heart can't save me from the water. So I slowly slip into the world of despair, undetected by the occupants of that dark world. I don't want to fight anymore, I've given in to darkness I've been pushed down so many times, I feel this time will be the last as I lay here fading my thoughts are invaded by memories of my past. I am physically weary, I am mentally depressed, I am spiritually defeated. I can't eat, can't sleep, I am like garbage, discarded refuse in the back alley, like yesterday's newspaper shuffled around by the wind. I feel like some sort of zombie, some non entity, some nothing that people, if they acknowledge, would only curse. No one hears me, understands me. I speak in silence hoping that someone will see my words, my message. I have no strength to get up, I'm not worth it anymore (Victim).

**(no title)**

Fondling, oral sex, he pretended to be teaching me about sex, intrusion on my privacy, belittling me as a female. He also physically and emotionally abused me. I told my mother. She said she did not think he was capable of such a thing. She asked exactly what kinds of things he did. Eventually, she said it was between he and I and she did not want to get involved. He was my step-father (Victim).

## The Frown From Inside

A blistering wind is focusing its invisible claws to an empty playground where the merry-go-round begins to spin. The squeaky ride picks up speed, and it becomes impossible to slow its progression. That's how my mind feels. I am, however, on the out-of–control ride and my journey traverses me into what I deem as madness.

I have passengers on my ride. As silly as it seems these characters are a part of me. I have attempted to travel without them, but they don't go away. They will remain behind the damp darkness if need be. Are they my friends? Certainly, but they have boundaries that are elastic. They will tempt me into inappropriate behavior. On the other hand, they have strength to assist me with daily troubles. Go figure.

So, the woman screams at the top of her lungs. It pierces my eardrums into horror. She is upset and it is her desperate desire to make certain that everyone knows it. The sweat on my brow is identical to the moisture creeping up on the back of my neck as my mind shuts down to the reality and it takes me back forty years.

Mommy, don't yell and slam the metal cabinet doors with hatred in your eyes. Your face becomes contorted and tight as each feature leaps to the maximum limit. Mommy, I'm here, don't be mad. Tell me what's wrong and I will make it go away, even if it hurts me. Even if it kills me. Remember mommy I am the sensitive one. You know I am. I've heard you tell your friends about me.

Eventually, you leave the house for awhile. What you left behind is a confused, gaunt feeling kid. That fear that I felt settles into my mind where I construct blueprints of either prompting pain onto others or myself. I'm slipping down a mineshaft, and the bottom of this pit welcomes me with a mattress of filth and sewage where my ideas simmer and contort. I could have helped. I could have. I could. I.................

One hour later all is well. The merry-go-round is now coming to a complete stop. My reality, and that of my alters is puzzled. We walk on paper thin glass that is already cracking. When will the next outburst occur? How will we react? Can I maintain a fractured amount of control, as we talked about? Who knows. My reactions are monitored by the very person who tosses out the madness. I feel as if I am back in a locked ward where apathetic professionals control my life. My well-being is no more important to them than how much butter they put on there toast each morning.

To top things off, the male voice uses my Lord's name in vain. It's like taking a shower in venom. Will I be cursed since I didn't rebuke him? It seems that there is a veil of evil surrounding all of us. I pray to my God and ask for guidance for the fog is quite thick and I would like to break through the barrier with His hand in mine.

My companions splinter off into their own worlds. I have agreements with them all to allow me to handle each situation no matter how uncomfortable it is. They have broken their promises in the past though. I'm not sure what bile is, but I think it is forming in my stomach.

I must remain vigilant. I must. If I become weary and fall asleep, I fear what might happen. One thing is certain. I have been both male and female voices in the past. I have scared the very ones I love.

This was more than a life lesson. It was life branding with a lasting reliance on proper daily living (Victim/Survivor).

**(no title)**

I only remember little parts like having to stay the night at my grandparents and my grandfather coming to my bed groping me at night. I remember learning if I touched him, he would not touch me and learned to not be alone in the day, but with Grandma or my brother. I did not know it was wrong which sounds crazy; just knew I did not like it (Victim).

**Disappointed**

When I was young I was molested by the person I truly trusted the most, my Grandpa. The whole situation put me in deep shock, that he would do such a thing, like this, to me, considering the fact that I was so close to him and my Grandma. He ruined the relationship between he and I and between me and my Grandma. I don't like him… Today I don't have any contact with him and very little contact with my Grandma. She chose him over her whole family. This makes me sad and confused, so I try not to think about it. I will someday (Victim).

**(no title)**

I told a women who was supposed to be my great grandmother and caregiver. I also told a lady who was supposed to be a great aunt. My great grandmother said I was making it up and then I was beaten mercilessly.

**Trying to Communicate**

(after parents find out that their 48 year old son is DID) Conflicting feelings surround my heart as I met my Dad on his home turf, his garage. Polite conversation followed and I noticed that the tension was tremendous. He spoke with wondering eyes, and twitches invaded his face. Was my presence so nerve racking? I saw the disappointment in his eyes as he surveyed me, his son, a mere stranger. His body language indicated a speck of fear as I attempted to follow the usual pattern of politeness. Please Dad, relax so I can not harbor split feelings about you. But no, You can't understand me, and I reckon that it's the same for me. I love you. I want to harm you. What will it take for you to accept me as I am. The roller coaster has jumped the tracks while this entire scenario spins out of control, like wildfires. Maybe your penance for accidentally being sloppy with your life juice is standing right in front of you. Does your heart break when you see what the dribble caused? Perhaps you have created your own incarceration, as the result of your lust stands before you, trembling inside and physically numb. I can't allow to let the laceration of my heart escape to the flesh. I have seen you more relaxed after having painful dentistry done. And each moment that we pretend to be happy, the more I feel like a grease stain on your perfectly kept garage floor, the pristine glory of your life standards. I have accepted the fact that you did the best you could with me growing up and you know that, so why increase your anxiety by excluding comfort from you for a few brief moments? Open your fucking eyes and focus on something positive. You can't, however, and you make idle comments that are intended to drill tiny holes into my mind. Guess what seeps in when you do that? (Victim/Survivor).

## (no title)

My uncle was caught in the act when I was 4. He was watched after that, but it was obvious it was not a topic for discussion. I didn't report the other abuses. My parents found out I was raped because I attempted suicide and the hospital informed them. I was told it wouldn't have happened if I would have been more careful and not to tell anyone.

## Be Honest

You say that you love me
But that is a lie
Don't worry about me
Cause soon I will die
You say that you care
But that is absurd
Cause everyone knows
Actions speak louder than words

But words can cut deep
As deep as a knife
And that is the reason
I'm taking my life
You say things to hurt me
You do your best
And I cry for hours
I guess you passed the test
Does it make you feel good
When you make me cry
Is that why we're together
Or do you even know why
I guess to be happy
Is too much to ask
And for you to show love
Is too hard to ask
You'll be glad when it's over
Relieved when I'm gone
You'll just find someone else
And you'll carry on
Well have a good life
It's time I must go
When they ask if you loved me
Be honest, say no (Victim).

**(no title)**

Molestation from brother included touching and oral
stuff, my brother always masturbating in front of family members and sexually abusing others, including
people that were in his special education class. There
were times when he would have a girl over from class
and take her in to the basement (which is where my
abuse occurred) and then letting the neighborhood

boys watch and participate in sexual ways. One of the times, to my greatest horror, the boys held the girl down as my brother urinated in her mouth...Mom would just come home from work and go to her room (Victim).

## My Comfort Drink

When days were bad, or I felt sad,
when I felt shame, and there was pain.
I'd ride my bike to the local store,
and drink my drink sitting on the floor,
or on the step. I must not leave, bottles cannot leave.
The taste of that cold "Big Red"
on a summers day, away from dread.
I drink it slow, they'll never know.
Unless, of course, it is time for one of his lessons,
the one's that "all daddy's must teach their little girls.
It's just our secret, don't ever tell, don't ever tell".
Is this normal, is this right, am I well?
When the lesson is over
I'll again become a roamer,
on my bike, to the local store,
drinking my "Big Red", sitting on the floor (Survivor/
Healer).

# BIBLIOGRAPHY

- Abramson, Paul R. (2001). *A House Divided: Suspicions of Mother-Daughter Incest.* New York: Norton.
- Adams, A. Brain Waves. Retrieved March 27, 2006, from http://mednews.stanford.edu/stanmed/2005fall/brain-main.html
- Adler, A. (1956). *The Individual Psychology of Alfred Adler.* New York: Harper & Row Publishers Inc.
- Alexander, P.C. (1993). The Differential Effects of Abuse: Characteristics and Attachment in the Prediction of Long Term Effects of Sexual Abuse. *Journal of Interpersonal Violence.* 8, 346-362.
- American Psychiatric Association. (2000). *Diagnostic and Statistical Manuel of Mental Disorders*, Fourth Edition Text Revision. Washington DC: The American Psychiatric Association.
- *APRI National Center for the Prosecution of Child Abuse*, Third Edition. (2004). Sage Publications: US.
- Bagley, C., Mallick, K., (Ed.). (1999). *Child Sexual Abuse & Adult Offenders: New Theory & Research.* Brookfield, VT: Ashgate Publishing Company.
- Bass, E., Davis, L. (1994). *The Courage to Heal.* New York: Harper Perennial.

- Bass, E., Davis, L. (1988). *The Courage to Heal – A Guide for Women Survivors of Child Sexual Abuse*. New York: Harper Perennial.

- Beitchman, J.H., Zucker, K.J., Hood, J.E., da Costa, G.A., & Akman, D. (1991). A Review of the Short Term Effects of Child Sexual Abuse. *Child Abuse and Neglect*. 15, 537-556.

- Boisset-Pioro, M.H., Esdaile, J.M., Fitzcharles, M.A. (1995). Sexual & Physical Abuse in Women with Fibromyalgia Syndrome. *Arthritis & Rheumatism*, 38, 235-241.

- Bremner, J.D. (1997). Magnetic Resonance Imaging Based Measurement of Hippocampal Volume in Posttraumatic Stress Disorder Related to Childhood Physical & Sexual Abuse, A Preliminary Report. *Biological Psychiatry*, 41, 23-32.

- Brown, D., Scheflin, A., Hammond, D.C., (1998). *Memory, Trauma, Treatment, and the Law*. New York: W.W. Norton & Company.

- Brunni, F. (2002). *A Gospel of Shame: Children, Sexual Abuse & The Catholic Church*. New York: Perennial.

- Burckhardt, C. (2004). Abuse & Fibromyalgia. Retrieved July 28, 2004, from http://www.myalgia.com/abuse.htm

- Cling, B.J., (ED), (2004). *Sexualized Violence Against Women and Children*. New York: The Guilford Press.

- Corsini, R., Wedding, D. (2005). *Current Psychotherapies*. Belmount, CA: Brooks/Cole - Thomas Learning Center.

- Courtois, C. (1988). *Healing the Incest Wound*. W.W. New York: Norton & Company.

- Dorais, M. (2002). *Don't Tell the Sexual Abuse of Boys*. Montreal: University Press.

- Douglas, J.E., Olshaker, M. (1997). *Journey Into Darkness*. Inc. New York: Simon & Schuster.

- Draucker, C.B. (1989). Cognitive Adaptation of Female Incest Survivors. *Journal of Consulting & Clinical Psychology*, 57(5), 668-670.

- Drossman, D., Leserman, J., Nachman, G., Li, Z., Gluck, H., Toomen, T., & Mitchell, M. (1990). Sexual and Physical Abuse in Women with Functional or Organic Gastrointestinal Disorders. *Annals of Internal Medicine*, 113, 828-833.

- Eby, D. (2004). Cognitive Accommodations to Childhood Sexual Abuse. Retrieved August 2, 2004 from http://www.talentdevelop.com/cogacc.html

- Ericksen, J.A. (2000). Sexual Liberations Last Frontier. *Society*, 37, 21-25.

- Felitti, V.J. (1991). Long Term Medical Consequences of Incest, Rape, & Molestation. *Southern Medical Journal*, 84, 328-331.

- Foa, E., Keane, T., Friedman, M. eds. (2000) *Effective Treatments For PTSD*. New York: The Guilford Press:.

- Forward, S. & Buck, C. (1989). *Toxic Parents*. New York: Bantam Books.

- Francher, R., (1973). *Psychoanalytic Psychology: The Development of Freud's Thought*. New York: Norton.

- Friedman, S. (1991). *Outpatient Treatment of Child Molesters*. Sarasota, FL: Professional Resource Exchange:.

- Fukunaga, T., Mizoi, Y., Yamashita, A., Yamada, M., Yamamoto, Y., Tatsuno, Y., Nishi, K. (1992).

Thymus of Abused/Neglected Children. *Forensic Science International,* 53, 69-79.

- Geer, J., Estupinan,M. & Manguno-Mire, G. (1999). Empathy, Social Skills and Other Relative Cognitive Processes in Rapist and Child Molesters. *Aggression and Violent Behavior,* 5, 99-126.

- Gladding, S. (1995). *Family Therapy: History, Theory, & Practice.* Englewood Cliffs, NJ: Prentice-Hall.

- Gladstone, G., Parker, G., Wilhelm, K., Mitchell, P., Marie-Paule, A. (1999). Characteristics of Depressed Patients Who Report Childhood Sexual Abuse. *The American Journal of Psychiatry,* 156, 431-437.

- Gorcey, M., Santiago, J.M., & McCall-Perez, F. (1986). Psychological Consequences for Women Sexually Abused in Childhood. *Social Psychiatry,* 21, 129-133.

- Harley Jr., W. (1986). *His Needs, Her Needs.* Grand Rapids, MI: Fleming H. Revell.

- Hamer, M. (2002). *Incest: A New Perspective.* Cambridge. UK: Polity Press.

- Harris, M. (2000). *Rape, Incest, Battery.* Fort Worth, TX: TCU Press.

- Hopper, J. (2004). Child Abuse Statistics, Research, and Resources, retrieved February 9, 2005 from www.jimhopper.com/abstracts

- Jones, J. (1997). *Kinsey: A Public/Private Life.* New York: WW Norton Inc.

- Keating, G. (2000). Disputed Theory Used in Custody Cases: Children Often Victims in Parental Alienation Syndrome Strategy. *Pasadena Star News.* April 23, 2000.

- Keith, J. (2005). Sex Experiments of Alfred Kinsey, retrieved February 3, 2005 from http://www.thetruthseeker.co.uk

- Kinsey, A., Pomeroy, W., Martin, C. (1948). *Sexual Behavior in the Human Male.* Philadelphia & London: W.B. Saunders Co.

- Kinsey, A., Pomeroy, W., Martin, C., Gebhard, P. (1953). *Sexual Behavior in the Human Female.* Philadelphia & London: W.B. Saunders Co.

- Kupelian, D. (2004). The Case Against Kinsey, retrieved February 3, 2005 from http://www.thetruthseeker.co.uk

- Kuyk, J., Spinhoven, P., VanEmdeBoas, W., VanDyck, R. (1999). Dissociation in Temporal Lobe Epilepsy & Pseudo-Epileptic Seizure Patients. *The Journal of Nervous and Mental Disease*, 187, 713-720.

- Lawson, D.M. (2001). The Development of Abusive Personality: A Trauma Response. *Journal of Counseling & Development*, 79, 505-509.

- Legal Information Institute: US Code Collection, Title 18, Part I, Chapter 109A, Section 2241.

- Lev, R. (1949). *Shine the Light: Sexual Abuse & Healing in the Jewish Community.* Boston: Northwestern University Press.

- Mandt, Langberg, D. M. (1997) *Counseling Survivors of Sexual Abuse.* Wheaton, IL: Tyndale House Publishers Inc.

- MacDonald, G., (1988). *Rebuilding Your Broken World.* Nashville, TN: Oliver Nelson.

- McCauley, J., Kern, D., Kolodner, K., Dill, L., Schroeder, A., DeChant, H., Ryden, J., Derogatis, L., Bass, E. (1997). Clinical Characteristics of Women with a History of Childhood Abuse: Unhealed Wounds. *Journal of the American Medical Association*, 277, 1362-1368.

- McGee, R. & Springle, P. (1992). *Getting Unstuck.* Dallas: Word Publishing.

- McKay, M., Davis, M., Franning, P. (1995). *Messages, The Communication Skills Book.* Oakland, CA: New Harbinger Publications Inc.

- Miller, D. (1994). *Women Who Hurt Themselves.* New York: Basic Books.

- Mullen, P.E., Martin, J.L., Anderson, J.C., Romans, S.E. & Herbison, G.P. (1996). The Long Term Impact of Physical, Emotional and Sexual Abuse of Children: A Community Study. *Child Abuse and Neglect*, 20,7-22.

- Naugle, A. (2004). Child Sexual Abuse Fact Sheet. Retrieved August 2, 2004, from http://www.nvaw. org/research/factsheet.shtml

- Parson, H. (2001). Child Abuse & Exploitation. Retrieved October 2, 2004, from http://www.hutchcc. edu/dept/4/

- Perry, B.D., Pollard, R., Blakely, T., Baker, W., Vigilante, D. (1996). Childhood Trauma, The Neurobiology of Adaptation & "Use-Dependent" Development of the Brain: How "States" Become "Traits". *Infant Mental Health Journal*, 16, 271-291.

- Phillips, A. & Daniluk, J.C. (2004). Beyond "Survivor": How Childhood Sexual Abuse Informs the Identity of Adult Women at the End of the Therapeutic Process. *Journal of Counseling & Development*, 82, 177-184.

- Pokrass, M. (2004). Adult and Adolescent Psychotherapy. Retrieved October 2, 2004, from http:// www.marionpokrasslcsw-c.com/

- Prescott, A. (2002). Childhood Abuse and the Potential Impact on Maternity. *Midwifery Matters*, 92, 17-18.
- Putman, F.W., & Trickett, P.K., (1997). Psychobiological Effects of Sexual Abuse: A Longitudinal Study. *Annals of the New York Academy of Sciences*, 821, 150-159.
- Reavey, P. & Warner, S. (2003). *New Feminist Stories of Child Sexual Abuse: Sexual Scripts & Dangerous Dialogues*. London: Routledge.
- Reisman, J. & Eichel (1990). Kinsey, Sex and Fraud. Department of Justice/Juvenile & Delinquency Prevention Report.
- Robson, P.J. (1988). Self Esteem-A Psychiatric View. *British Journal of Psychiatry*. 153, 6-15.
- Russell, D. E. (1986). *The Secret Trauma – Incest in the Lives of Girls and Women*. New York: Basic Books Inc.
- Sagatun, I. & Edwards, L. (1995). *Child Abuse and the Legal System*. United States: Wadsworth.
- Seamonds, D. (1985). *Healing Memories*. Victor Books: Wheaton, IL.
- Schaumburg, H. (1997). *False Intimacy*. Colorado Springs, CO: NAVPress.
- Schlesinger, L.B., (ED), (2000). *Serial Offenders: Current Thought, Recent Findings*. Library of Congress, USA: CRC Press LLC.
- Schnurr, P. (2004). The Effects of Traumatic Stressor Exposure on Physical Health. Retrieved July 28, 2004, from http://www.dcha.org/EP/Articles/The%20 Effects%20of%20Traumatic%20% Stressor%20Ex.htm
- Schofferman, J., Anderson, D., Hinds, R., Smith, G., White, A. (1992). Childhood Psychological Trauma Correlates With Unsuccessful Lumbar Spine Surgery. *Spine*, 17, S1381-S1384.

- Sidran Foundation. (2003). About Trauma. Retrieved October 13, 2003 from http://www.sidran.org/didbr. html

- Silver, R.L., Boon, C. & Stones, M.H. (1983). Searching for Meaning in Misfortune: Making Sense of Incest. *Journal of Social Issues*, 39(2), 81-101.

- Silverman, J. (2002). *Innocence Betrayal: Pedophilia, the Media & Society*. UK: Cambridge.

- Socarides, C.W. & Loeb, L.R., (EDs.), (2004). *The Mind of the Pedophile: Psychoanalytic Perspectives*. London & New York: Karnac.

- Springle, P. (1994). *Trusting*. Servant Publications: Ann Arbor, MI.

- Stark, E. & Holly, Marshall. *Everything You Need to Know About Sexual Abuse*. New York: The Rosen Publishing Group.

- Taylor, C. (1991). *The Inner Child Workbook*. New York: Penguin Putman Inc.

- Taylor, M.L., Trotter, D.R., Csuka, M.E. (1995). The Prevalence of Sexual Abuse in Women with Fibromyalgia. *Arthritis & Rheumatism*, 38, 229-234.

- Teegen, F.. (Eds.), (1999). Post Traumatic Stress Disorder: A Lifespan Developmental Perspective. (97-112). Seatle: Hogrefe & Huber.

- The Awareness Center. (2004). History of Child Abuse, Neglect, and Sexual abuse/Assault Laws. Retrieved February 21, 2006 from http://www.theawareness-center.org/HistoryChildAbuse.html

- White Kress, V.E. (2003). Self-Injurious Behaviors: Assessment & Diagnosis. *Journal of Counseling & Development*, 81, 490-496.

- Whitlock, K. & Gillman, R. (1989). Sexuality: A Neglected Component of Child Sexual Abuse Education. *Child Welfare*, 68, 317-329.

- Wiehe, V. R. (1997). *Sibling Abuse: Hidden Physical, Emotional, and Sexual Trauma.* Thousand Oaks, California: Sage Publications.

- Wikipedia. (2006). History of Child Sexual Abuse as a Social Problem. Retrieved February 21, 2006 from http://en.wikipedia.org

- Wilson, S. (2001). *Hurt People Hurt People.* Grand Rapids, MI; Discovery House Publishers.

- Wonderlich, S. (2000). Child Sexual Abuse, Disclosure. *Journal of the American Academy of Child and Adolescent Psychiatry*, 39, 1277-1283.

# APPENDIX I

# INTERVIEW QUESTIONS FOR CRIMINAL JUSTICE PERSONNEL

1) Approximately how many Child Sexual Abuse cases are investigated in this county per year?

2) Of those cases, how many get to trial?

3) What is the nature of the abuse investigated?

4) How do you think the legal process affects the children?

5) Is reunification of the family a primary goal?

6) Who is responsible for these children getting counseling?

7) Do the children usually have a good support system around them?

8) Do you investigate the past of the offender for other victims?

9) What is your opinion of recovered memories and how is that treated, from a legal standpoint?

10) Do you think Child Molesters are treatable?

11) Do you think that our current laws punish offenders proportionately to the nature of their crime?

12) Do you see a "ripple effect" of any kind through the families of victims and/or society in general?

*9798890794178*